Marion Soep

Our Sister Sahib

with Foreword by Sir Eric Yarrow
and
Introduction by David Carnduff

To Carol

Marn Soep

ISBN-10: 0-9551893-0-6
ISBN-13: 978-0-9551893-0-2

Produced by
New Vision Print and Publishing Ltd
43A Esplanade
Greenock
PA16 7RY

Tel. 01475 783000   Fax 01475 728145
Website www.newvisionpublishing.co.uk
E-mail enquiries@newvisionpublishing.co.uk

Printed and bound by
J H Haynes and Co Ltd
Yeovil
Tel. 01963 440635

Dedication

In memory of Bernard Soep
and
my Indian Ward Boys

The lance corporal (a Brahmin) and the others
(Hindu, Muslim and Untouchable)

Contents

(*articles published elsewhere by Bernard Soep)

Foreword

As President of the Burma Star Association in Scotland, I have had the pleasure of knowing Mrs Marion Soep. She is an active member of the Association and has shown great enterprise and courage in taking part in a visit to the battlefields of Burma recently.

Her book is a fascinating account of very commendable work both in times of peace and war. Many ex-service men and women have benefited from her great kindness, skill and devotion to duty and must be very grateful for her outstanding nursing services, often carried out in difficult and dangerous conditions.

I have no hesitation in recommending her most interesting book and in keeping with her character, profits raised from selling her book will go to the Ardgowan Hospice in Greenock.

Sir Eric Yarrow
Kilmacolm, June 2005

Acknowledgements

I would like to offer sincere and heartfelt thanks to the following people, without whom this book would not have been written or published:

My sons John and Roger and their families – for typing and all manner of support over many years.

Sir Eric Yarrow – for taking the time out from a busy schedule to read early excerpts of the manuscript and checking the accuracy of the campaign details as well as spending time to write the Foreword.

Burma Star Association – for kind permission to use the Association Logo and Historical Note.

The *Nautical Magazine* – for kind permission to allow reprinting of the stories written by my late husband, Captain Bernard Soep: "Treason on the High Seas", "The Miracle", "Hospital Ship No. 6" and "The Chart" – and especially Mr Brown, the Editor, for his kind encouragement.

St. Bartholomew's Hospital, London, and especially Katie Ormerod (Assistant Archivist) and Miranda Hungerford (Work Experience Student) – for hunting down and supplying the graduation photograph.

Norman Burniston and *Greenock Telegraph* – for kind permission to use two photographs from their archive.

Jane Cox – for early computer advice, panic control and always being there when needed.

David Carnduff – for writing the Introduction, and for initial organisation and editorial advice coupled with the composition of all matters relating thereto.

Ardgowan Hospice – for organising and dealing with all aspects relating to marketing of this book as well as undaunted support.

Eleanor Ogilvie – for typing and computer tuition plus my introduction to Lead Scotland.

Lead Scotland – for organisation of home study and tuition.

Andrew Steen – for computer tuition at home coupled with encouragement over a hard three months.

James Watt College – for assistance in the preparation of aspects of the book and computer tuition.

Stephen Callaghan – for long months of tuition, encouragement, major editorial effort and kindness throughout.

Paul Bristow – for first fix organisation and early proof reading.

Jean Galbraith – for editing duties and advice as well as encouragement.

Chris Jewell – for the control and supervision of all matters relating to publication.

Alison Black – for accurate reading and printing preparation.

Bernard Simon – for producing the electronic file.

Kathy Tattersall – for producing the illustrations.

New Dawn Bookshop – for assistance and advice in all matters relating to publication.

Three Anonymous Good Friends – for funding support and encouragement throughout – you know who you are.

The University of Texas Libraries, the University of Texas at Austin – for permission to use their maps.

Martin Thomas – for photographic services.

Arthur Wilkins – for everything that was necessary when required, including crisis management.

And to all the husbands, wives, girlfriends, partners, sons and daughters who have missed their respective soul mates as a result of my constant need for assistance of all kinds at all times of the day and night, which has required the prolonged absence from your side of your loved ones – thank you for your patience and understanding in often very trying circumstances.

If in the course of preparation of these acknowledgements I have omitted anyone, please accept my heartfelt thanks and apology.

Marion Soep
Greenock, October 2005

Introduction

By David Carnduff

For Marion Soep, life has been nothing short of an adventure. At 5 ft, 1 in., her diminutive appearance belies a huge appetite for life; a life she has crammed with a kaleidoscope of rich experiences, and one predominately dedicated towards the care of others.

Now in her 90s, the adventure continues. For despite suffering from a degenerative eye disease, Marion has used her seemingly limitless reserves of energy and enthusiasm to write this account of some of her profound experiences.

And there is much to choose from in a life which includes a long and distinguished career as a nurse and midwife, her involvement with the Girl Guide movement and her long association with Ardgowan Hospice in Greenock.

But especially poignant, in this year of the Diamond Jubilee of V.J. Day, are her memories from the Burma Campaign when she nursed hundreds of wounded soldiers, including Japanese prisoners-of-war, who had fallen victim of the long and bloody war fought in the malaria ridden jungles of South East Asia.

Marion and her colleagues in the Queen Alexandra's Imperial Military Nursing Service coped admirably with the difficult conditions and poor medical equipment in Casualty Clearing Stations. But it was hard and demanding work and Marion herself fell ill with amoebic dysentery.

Sent to recuperate in Darjeeling, 7,000 feet up in the Himalayas, Marion realised the sojourn in the cool, clear mountain air was another opportunity for adventure. Once on her feet again, she set off – with her own personal Sherpa – to explore the astonishing beauty of the world's highest mountain range, getting into one or two scrapes along the way, but none that she and her trusted Sherpa were unable to overcome.

It was an experience that whetted her appetite for the Himalayas and she returned towards the end of the war on another trip, this time with the handsome young Chief Officer whom she would marry.

Marion's adventurous traits first appeared many years earlier when childhood escapades indicated that she was a tomboy through and through. Born in Woodford, Essex, in 1913 to George William Roger and Marion Hetherington, she was the youngest of four children. Jane, the eldest, was thirteen years older to the day (she and Marion shared the same birthday), Mary was next at eleven years older and the only boy, George, was six when Marion was born.

Marion has no doubts she should have been a boy. She was fanatical about horses and ships, and it is no surprise that she was very close to her father who owned a shipbuilding and engineering yard in Irvine,

Ayrshire before moving South with his family to manage a large shipyard in London.

As she progressed through school and thought about a career, Marion variously considered going to sea, or being a vet or a doctor. At 19 she decided on a career in nursing, so it was in February 1933 that she started training at the historic St Bartholomew's Hospital in Smithfield, London. Times were hard, poverty and poor housing meant St Barts wards were always filled to overflowing, but the hospital was an excellent training ground for Marion.

Later she qualified as a midwife and the future looked rosy. But war was looming and Marion's life was about to change dramatically.

Here, in a series of delightful reminiscences, Marion takes up the story ...

1

Early Days and St Barts

Formative years: 1913–1933
Midwifery training, Radcliffe Hospital, Oxford:
April–November 1937
Midwife, Cape Town, South Africa: Spring
1938–September 1939

My father, William, hailed from Aberdeen originally and by the 1890s, being a naval architect and shipbuilder by profession, was owner and M.D. of the Irvine Shipbuilding Yard in the Ayrshire town of Irvine. Having met and married my Glasgow born mother Marion in 1889, they settled in the county town of Ayr where my two elder sisters were born, Jane in 1900 and Mary in 1902.

In 1903, due to changes in the shipbuilding industry, my father took up the position of M.D. of another shipyard in the South of England, which meant a family move to Woodford in Essex, where my brother George was born in 1904. I, being the last and naturally the youngest in the family, was born on 8 October 1913 in Woodford, Essex. I have no recollection of this house, as several months later the family moved to a new home in Blackheath, London.

My father was a great one for telling stories and describing incidents that had highlighted his varied life, particularly in the shipbuilding and engineering industries. One of the stories which comes to mind relates to the owner of a large coal company who commissioned the building of a ship by my father's Irvine shipyard. The ship subsequently sank not long after hand-over, causing the owner to sue my father's company. The matter eventually ended in the High Court in Edinburgh. My father had a model of the ship built and a tank of water placed in the court room. Using the assistance of his Q.C., he managed to demonstrate that the cause of the tragedy was the way the coal had been loaded and not defective construction. My father was nobody's fool.

In later years, when my father had retired, he became involved with the Shaftesbury Homes, similar to Quarriers Homes, which owned and operated a sailing vessel called the T.S. *Arethusa,* which had been converted into a school for boys wishing to enter the Royal or Merchant Navy. About 1931 the T.S. *Arethusa* had to be replaced due to old age and the S.S. *Peking*, which was the largest four-masted steel barque in the world at that time, was bought from a German company. The S.S. *Peking* had been trading from Europe to the West Coast of South America, which meant twice round the Horn each trip in all weathers. My father was approached and, offered the opportunity to carry out the conversion of this new purchase; he jumped at the chance, and by using unemployed shipyard workers in Falmouth the S.S. *Peking* was completely altered to accommodate a gymnasium, dormitories, classrooms and a chapel. When completed she was towed and moored at Upnor on the river Medway, at which point the name was changed to the T.S. *Arethusa*. In June 1933 there was a special opening ceremony held with H.R.H. Prince George doing the honours. I was invited but unfortunately was unable to attend as by that time I had just started my nursing training and was terrified to ask for a day off ... Oh, what a pity.

Forty years later the T.S. *Arethusa* was deemed no longer suitable and was reluctantly put up for sale by auction. As she was by now the largest steel sailing ship afloat in the world, the Shaftesbury Homes made every possible attempt to raise funding to keep the ownership of the vessel in the U.K., but the old ship was purchased by the Seaport Museum in New York and, having been towed across the Atlantic, was restored to its original state as the S.S. *Peking*. From the proceeds of the sale a ketch was commissioned and built by the Shaftesbury Homes and named the T.S. *Arethusa* to commemorate the original. Since then this ship has been sold on to a school for disadvantaged children, but, alas, Shaftesbury Homes would not allow the name to go with the sale.

So there you are, my father and grandfather before him were inspirations to me in my formative years, which might go some way to explain my 'tomboy' nature, more of which will no doubt be referred to later as this chronicle of my experiences unfolds ... Now where was I? Oh, yes.

I was educated partly at Blackheath High School and later at the Downs, a small boarding school near Brighton where there were many interesting activities, including Girl Guides. The headmistress was many years ahead of her time. We had a school council made up of representatives from each form and all of the sixth form. They had considerable responsibilities and at the end of the term we had a school parliament. We had a number of foreign girls for short periods, which made life very interesting. We thoroughly enjoyed producing plays and attending concerts.

I had always wanted to be a nurse and my ambition was fulfilled in 1933 when I entered St Bartholomew's Hospital, London (St Barts or Barts), where I had first-class training. I started my training on 1 February at the age of 19 years and four months, a year younger than was usual. Matron thought that I was enthusiastic and could manage. That has been a problem with my superiors all my life. My mother came with me to the primary training school. This was in Queen's Square, Goswell Road in the City of London. I was welcomed in as Nurse and the first job was to embroider my name on a Barts cloak. If we were not accepted at the end of eight weeks the last job was to unpick the embroidery!

The training was basic nursing, and there was only *one* way to make a Barts bed. I had learned a certain number of skills in the Guides, but the only thing that was the same was using what we called "Guide corners" when making a bed. Most of our group had some nursing experience, but they had to do the same as those without any experience. One was a fully

11

trained children's nurse and she had taken the preliminary state exam, but that made no difference. The idea seemed to be that you had to train again at Barts. We finished our eight weeks, we had our exam, and the only subject that could be sat again was cooking. Strangely enough I passed that. The examiner could not have seen how long my scones had been in the oven. Perhaps she was impressed with my enthusiastic scrubbing of the wooden boards.

Those who were fortunate moved into the hospital to start as probationers. The nurses home was fairly new and we had single rooms with a large wardrobe with drawers and plenty of shelves. We were all together and there was a little space with a hot plate and a kettle where we could make some snacks. There were marvellous baths, which we could revel in when we came off duty. We were called at six o'clock in the morning, the maid who looked after us banging on every door, shouting, "Six o'clock, nurse!" If we were not on duty we put our name label up so we were left in peace. It was wonderful to be able to lie tucked up in bed and listen to the doors being knocked and the wake-up call shouted and know that you could have a long lie. We could have our breakfast in bed if we signed a book for a yes, please! That was magic. At eight o'clock there was a knock at the door and a lovely tray was brought in including a cooked breakfast and a pot of tea. It was bliss. If we were off sick the sick rooms were very pleasant and we were well looked after, but we had to do as we were told. We were the only nursing teaching hospital where the nurses had a day off each week with the evening off before. We had to be in by ten o'clock but could have a midnight pass once a month. This increased later. If we were off duty in the evening there were often some theatre tickets offered and we were given a pass.

The big day arrived and we started as probationers in our first ward. I started in Sandhurst Ward, the medical professors' ward, and I was the relief probationer nurse. I worked with Staff Nurse Way, 'The Belt' (the nickname for a fully qualified nurse). She was a wonderful nurse and teacher, and what she taught me has stayed with me to this day. She let me work at my own pace; perhaps she thought that I had potential. I was slow but very thorough and rather stubborn. I did not like to leave a job until I felt that it was correct. I always remember a young boy with rheumatic fever and he was not allowed to move a finger to prevent heart damage, which would affect him all his life. Nurse Way worked with me until she felt I could manage by myself. Nurse Way later became a doctor.

When I relieved the probationer in the front ward on her day off I must have driven the poor 'stripe' (2nd or 3rd year nurse) demented as I was always about ten minutes behind. After the patients were washed and the beds made, the beds were pulled out along with the curtains, then the cleaning ladies moved in and the entire ward was swept. My senior dusted the back of the beds and the little medicine shelf on the wall, then the curtains were quickly folded in a special way and slapped back in place. At this time I was to dust the patients' lockers and polish the linoleum side of the locker mats. I always spent too much time, but they had to be done to my satisfaction!

There was one very special patient that I will never forget: his name was Pearson, and he was in bed 13, near to the sister's desk. He had rheumatoid arthritis in every joint in his body, so when we made his bed it took ages to arrange pillows supporting every joint to leave him as comfortable as possible. When it was my turn to give him a blanket bath it was a privilege, and I had lots of jokes with him. The first time I did not know how to cope with false teeth and rushed to get advice; the answer was, "Just catch them!"

On the second Wednesday of May each year it was View Day and the hospital was open for viewing to various people. The Sisters went to Covent Garden to buy flowers at a very early hour in the morning; the ward tables had looking glass tops and the flowers looked very special. In the morning the Lord Mayor and his retinue went round the whole hospital on inspection, speaking to the Sister and giving the nurses a nod. We were the only hospital in the city. In the afternoon the nurses could invite their families to come to tea. My mother and father both came and I was thrilled. While they were sitting, my father looked down the ward and saw a patient that he recognised. He went down and shook his hand and greeted him by name. He remembered him as a shipwright in the shipyard of which he had been managing director, several years before. He sat on the locker and talked of the old times when it had been a family business and the workforce had been father and son over the years.

The old man was so happy and never stopped telling me how wonderful it was that the boss remembered him after all those years. He had a very serious heart condition and he died the next week, but happy.

My three months was up and Sister called me into her room. This was the moment of truth. She told me to sit down and then said that she was electing me but there was just one thing: "In a men's ward, when there are screens round a bed and I hear with my ears peels of laughter ... oh, nurse, it *does not do, in a men's ward!*" Needless to say the patient in question was dear old Pearson in bed 13.

I was very lucky. I had loved working under a Sister who ran a happy and busy ward with a professor of medicine using all sorts of new treatments. I think that Sister had been pleased with my efforts at turning out her store cupboard, which took me a long time. I was able to do the job to my satisfaction!

Now to the ceremony of Elections. Our whole group were assembled together, our uniforms immaculate, sitting in a room opening on to the Great Hall where the Matron, Senior Consultant and Governor sat below the huge Hogarth oil paintings of Jesus healing the sick and disabled. We were called in alphabetical order and asked to sit down. If we had not been elected, a second chance might be offered in another ward. Failing that, the probationer went out of the building, packed her bags, unpicked her embroidery on her cloak and went home. The lucky ones had a celebration in our quarters. All our group were successful and finished their training – we were in!

Every three months there was a change of wards for the nursing staff unless it was moving from the ward to night duty. I went on night duty as relief mostly in the medical wards. I started in the eye ward and spent much time cleaning things in the eye theatre.

On the last night I thought that the Night Sister's final visit to the nurse-in-charge was rather long. When we went to breakfast there was a notice stating that that nurse had been dismissed for sleeping on duty. That was the end of her career – apparently she was found asleep on cushions with screens all around her. That was the only sad experience that I met. The probationer whose nights off I was doing was very distressed and criticised me for not rousing my superior. I told her that she had not put it on my list of duties!

The next three months it was to the new surgical block, Rees-Mogg Ward. The senior surgeon did the very latest chest surgery, which carried a considerable risk, which he always explained to his patients. On my first day in the ward he came in and did not have a white coat on or a label with his name – I told him to sit on a chair at the door until the sister could be consulted. When she saw him and was told that this little nurse would not let him in she turned on me, but he stopped her and said that it was his fault. After that I always got a special smile. Some time later he lost his right hand with blood poisoning caused by a prick through his glove when operating on a badly infected lung. Later, as he was no longer able to operate in the theatre, he was planning to switch to a career as a physician, but

16

sadly he died ...we had no antibiotics in those days ... what a brave man!

One evening, when it was nearly time for Sister to say prayers, I had to move a table to the place where the light could be pulled down and a shield put round it for the night pro to work. One of the wheels was sticking and I tipped the table to fix it. There was an ear-splitting crash as the looking glass top fell to the floor. A voice from a male patient remarked, "Someone dropped their false teeth?"

The breakage book was taken to the Matron on Friday mornings. So that was my job that week. "Well, nurse, if you had to pay for that breakage it would cost £20, a year's salary!" That was my introduction to the surgical wards and it was followed by three months of night relief. I started with four nights in Rees-Mogg where I had been working.

After three months with the Sister in Rees-Mogg Ward where I learnt my surgical skills, the next three were spent on night duty, again relieving four surgical wards which included Paget Ward. Sister gave me all my instructions.

I was shown how to lay the trolley for any dressings if needed. There were two sterilisers, one small for instruments and a large one. The sterilisers were filled with water and brought to the boil with steam. There was a wooden board on which to put the boiling hot china dishes. Sister laid a linen cloth on the glass trolley; she made the point that the hot dishes would break the glass. Needless to say I was careful to carry out these instructions.

When I went relief in Paget Ward on the same floor but opposite, when the night pro was on her nights off, the Sister gave me all my instructions, but she lifted the hot dishes straight on to the cloth covered glass trolley. I shouted "No! You will break the glass!" Sister looked at me in amazement and said very firmly, "Nurse, my trolleys *never* break." When our group of graduates of 1937 visited Rees-Mogg Ward for a Reunion and A.G.M. many years later, we visited these two Sisters and I told them of my experience with the trolleys, they were highly amused. No one had ever told them! I suppose in those days we did not dare.

We always kept a double boiler filled with milk ready if a patient needed a hot drink; skin always formed on the top and we skimmed it off into a cup. Later we whisked it up and we would have Devonshire cream to put on our pudding.

Our seniors let the two pros (nickname for probationers) have a little time together. When the patients were settled we had to clean everything in the sluices – basins, sinks and so on – and steep the stainless steel bedpans in Lysol, and then we had to polish them with soap pads. One of the jokes we used to have was to compete with the other pros on Paget Ward to see which of us had the most highly polished bedpans.

We were fortunate, these wards were near the top of the building and in the early morning the sight of the sunrise over Saint Paul's Cathedral was very special.

On night duty we worked from 8.00 p.m. for twelve hours, having breakfast at 7.30 p.m. The pro collected a tin with food for the night. The probationer had to prepare a meal about 11.00 p.m., perhaps bacon and egg. Some Sisters left something to add to the meal. My efforts were rather pathetic, but the tea at 4.00 a.m. was prepared by the senior and I was lucky in usually sitting down to a tasty tea.

We could not start treatments too early, and then breakfast, which was simple except on Sundays when it was bacon and eggs for 24 people. This was the probationer's job. In one ward I had a chef as a patient and he taught me a way – boiling water poured over eight eggs in a bowl, left a minute then broken into the bowl then slipped into the frying pan, so no broken yolks!

The day staff came on at 7.30 and we did some washings and then off to our dinner at 8.00 a.m. and to bed. There were three Night Sisters who did several rounds and more if there was a problem.

On night duty we had four nights off after twelve on nightshift, which gave us a little break. On several occasions my father let me have the use of the family car, which I had collected the day before. My great friend was Mazie Calcutt, and she lived in Islip, a village a few miles outside Oxford. Without a thought we set off after our meal and drove to our destination. It was a old farm house with quite a bit of land. It lay beside the river, and of course there was a lot to do and see in Oxford.

The end of our first year and the exam – this was the next hurdle. Happily, all our set passed and then came the big moment: changing into our stripe uniforms.

Now we would have a probationer to look after and teach.

We had a chart that we had to hand to the Sister of the ward where we worked. When we had been shown a treatment it was ticked, and when we were proficient it was marked. This made sure that we had covered everything. My theatre experience was in a little theatre on the top floor beside Radcliffe Ward for infected wounds. It was fascinating because I had all the old equipment from the old theatres, beautiful copper drums and my own small autoclave, which I had to use to sterilise dressings and other things. This was a great help to me later when on the hospital ship.

I spent six months in Waring Ward, first on days. It was a female ward at that time. Sister was a wonderful nurse, but she had a bad temper if you annoyed her (she was from Aberdeen and was thrifty!). It never worried me if I was learning. 'The Belt' was Dainty, now Mrs Rabin Williams. The senior stripe was Woodruff Hill and there were two grand pros. We were a great team and always helped each other. It was a very busy ward and we saw a lot of accidents, especially being so near to Smithfield market. We had one memorable case, a Mrs Field who had been knocked down by a horse and cart. One leg was on weights to the pulley above the bed to give traction to the leg. It took several of us to do her back. I was the smallest, and while the others lifted I had to dress the injuries on her back, and had to be quick about it. While at the same A.G.M. I mentioned earlier, the group of us were surprised to find that the ward was now a male ward, and as I was reminiscing about the story of Mrs Field once more I said, "Good gracious, that was thirty years ago." An elderly patient sitting on his bed and listening with interest commented, "My word, you have all worn well!"

When I went on night duty on the ward along with my pro, Nurse Cruikshanks, it was hectic. I had to sit at the table when I was not attending to patients; here I could see most of the ward. I had various treatments to do. The desk had a pile of linen that was to be repaired. Each article had blue pencil drawn round the part to be patched. A pillowcase usually had each corner marked! If the surgeon was on call there would be emergency admissions. Then there was the rush to be finished in time for the day staff. The two of us were the last to reach the dining room for our dinner and we would receive a clap.

I had an operation to remove my tonsils after several doses of tonsillitis and was a patient in my ward, thoroughly spoiled.

Finally the big day came and we sat our final exam. There were no resits permitted, so we were all busy with last minute study. Our ward reports were of considerable importance. I was very encouraged when even Sister Waring wished me luck. Once again, all our set were successful and with pride we pinned on our Barts badges and a friend tied our blue belt round our waist. We were now considered to be fully qualified – though we still had to sit the state exam during the year.

Now we would spend six months in two different wards or departments. I started in the E.N.T. Department and worked with Sir Sidney Scot; he was a wonderful person and taught me everything that I had to perform. He arrived late one morning, dressed in morning coat with stiff white cuffs. He had just been called to attend the Duke and Duchess of York at Buckingham Palace as Princess Margaret Rose had a sore throat. The next six months were spent in a medical ward; this was a very demanding time. When the Sister was off duty I was entirely responsible. In the summer the Sisters were on holiday for a whole month: that meant being in charge for all that period with no days off! The Sister of the ward on the same floor was very helpful and offered to stand in for me if I wanted to go out. She never interfered, though I was welcome to ask for advice. I had the privilege of going to Sister's breakfast at eight o'clock. The consultant was very helpful and rather enjoyed making me feel important. This experience was excellent as we were made to be responsible and were able to take charge when we were working in the big wide world. It has stood me in good stead during my career, sometimes to my superior's surprise and occasionally ... concern!

Most of our patients were poor, and it was a privilege to spoil them, and particularly if they were female – we would get nice nightclothes for them.

The hospital was a teaching hospital and had funding committees, which supplied special things – beautiful bedspreads with the crest in the middle, and pink decorations in the women's wards and blue in the men's.

Christmas was very special; the students gave concerts over some weeks and on Christmas day.

During day duty in Rees-Mogg Ward, it was stockings and Santa Claus and Christmas dinner with the consultant carving the turkey in the ward. There was no off duty and we ate our dinner in the dining room. In the afternoon our families could join us and we had great fun.

One or two of our set went far, in particular Joan Loveridge who ended as Matron of Barts and never lost her sense of humour and fun; sadly she died well before her time. I remember the hilarious times we had when we were in Oxford doing our midwifery.

I do not think that modern nurses have such happy and amusing stories to tell. We worked very hard but had great rewards. Some of the nurses of those times will have similar stories. We were all proud to have a Barts training. Sadly it is no longer a training school, but is doing a great job for cancer patients.

We were expected to take midwifery training and a group of us went to the Radcliffe Hospital in Oxford. Because we were part of the hospital, we did not have a matron but a sister in charge. That was Sister Aldous, who was the most up-to-date and wonderful teacher, also Barts trained. We were the last group to train in six months; I think we did about 90 hours a week.

The first lecture was by a local consultant and he told us that we were training to deliver babies, that we would be the experts and that he would never dream of delivering a baby in front of a midwife. Consultants were only called in for surgical emergences.

We had to get bicycles as we would be working out in the district during part of our training. I did not expect to see so much poverty in a country place, but every three out of five men were out of work. Towards the end of our training when we did our work on district, we each had to attend ten deliveries during that time. There were several students and we were on a rota, so when it was night duty we were called and had to be up, dressed and in the duty room, eating a sandwich, taking the notes, looking at the map and then on to the bikes and off at speed. We were rather like firemen; your clothes were all laid out in order. We rode through the dark streets in perfect safety – what a difference from today. We had to assess the situation, make sure that the husband had pennies for the phone and the hospital number when you needed the midwife. It was quite a responsibility.

On one occasion it was a comfortable home and a very special first baby. I was urgently needing the midwife's advice and felt rather panic stricken – the baby's cord was caught around her neck. However, I suddenly remembered what to do and delivered a lovely baby girl; there was great rejoicing. Another time, there was an urgent call and the midwife and I went together. It was an old house soon to be knocked down, and the husband met us at the door to say that the baby had already arrived. No electricity, so bike lamps and candles were in order. The couple had been at a boxing match and had to make a hurried departure. This was number thirteen, with a year between each! We bathed the baby – a big one! – and made a cradle up out of a drawer. There were two bedrooms in which there were two beds for four children, the rest in cots, again each holding two. Fred, the father, was a driver of a coal lorry. Whenever he passed me on my bike, I would get a big wave. They were a lovely family, poor but contented. I kept in touch for some time. I wrote to her from India and she replied asking what could she send me!

We did evening rounds in villages some miles away. In these areas there was again considerable poverty; hardly a single man was employed, but the women were wonderful: you only had to put your head out of the window and call out to borrow a blanket or anything. I had a very kind uncle who owned Creamola, the dessert manufacturers, and so all my district mothers were sent a parcel of groceries.

While I was there I read a letter in the Barts journal from a nurse who was working in Kentucky with the mounted nursing service in the Blue Mountains. I could not believe that such a wonderful job could be possible. I wrote off for all the particulars and the conditions were strict. You required district nurse training followed by two years district nursing in the Scottish highlands. I asked Sister Aldous's advice, she went away and the next day said that she thought that it was just the very job for me. Perhaps she had watched me jumping on to my bike. There would be no need for me to go to Scotland; she would see that I had the necessary experience with her. That sounded wonderful, but I had promised to take a holiday job in Yorkshire near a cousin who had recently lost her husband. When my father heard of my scheme he had a fit. "Go to America, good gracious? Who won the war?" I am quite sure that he asked my sister Mary in South Africa to invite me to stay and help her as she was expecting another baby. He obviously agreed to pay my fare.

So it was that I sailed to Cape Town on a visit that would last a year. The idea was that I could help with her little boy while she had another baby. What a grand place to live: swimming, picnics on beautiful beaches, climbing the mountains and lots of horse riding. There was a shortage of midwives so I was sometimes busy, but there was terrible poverty and poor treatment of Coloureds.

They had to sit on separate seats everywhere. There were different times for them. I remember one incident when a young white student was in District 6, the coloured area. He assaulted the wife of a pub owner and he was pushed away by the husband. He went home and returned with a gun and shot the husband. The court just let him off with a warning as he had his career to think of.

On 3 September 1939, I was with a case near Table Mountain when war was declared. I had planned a wonderful trip up the coast and a visit to one of the wildlife parks, but this had to be abandoned because South Africa initially did not declare war and I was determined to go home. The German pocket battleship *Graf Spee* was sinking ships and rescuing the crews but then made the mistake of sinking the S.S. *Africa Shell*. That brought the South African government into the war. By the time that we left, the British Navy had cornered the *Graf Spee* in the harbour at Montevideo and the Captain scuttled her. He and his crew became prisoners.

Despite urgent messages from my father to stay where I was, I set off home on the S.S. *City of Nagpur*, the same ship that I had come out on. My brother-in-law, John Hollingdale, approved of my decision to go home but he insisted, however, that I should have a deck cabin. I was one of three ladies sailing on the *City of Nagpur* and the ship's master, Captain Lloyd, assured him the three lady passengers on board would, indeed, have deck cabins – and he would take as good care of us as possible.

There was one elderly lady called Hess. Later we wondered if she was related to Rudolf Hess. The other was a young girl going to Freetown in West Africa to marry a naval officer.

By the time that we approached Freetown she was beginning to have doubts and sought reassurance from the Captain, Chief Engineer and myself who had become her nearest and dearest. She was a gorgeous bride and the groom was a very handsome young man. The church was small and the heat terrific. When the service was half way through, I realised she was about to fall and pushed a chair under her. She was given a drink of water and the padre went back to the beginning of the Promise. Afterwards, we had a very magnificent repast supplied by the Navy. I never heard how things turned out for the bride and groom.

Now we had to sail home through more dangerous waters. I wanted a job aboard ship to keep me occupied and Captain Lloyd was more than ready to make use of my services as a look out. So, dressed in oilskins and sou'wester, I scrambled up into the 'monkey' bridge and scoured the horizon with binoculars for any vessels – feeling rather important. Halfway through my 'watch' a sailor came up with a mug of hot cocoa wrapped in a cloth. I enjoyed my spells and I thought that I was adequately disguised as a sailor but the Convoy Commandant signalled a message asking if the lady on look out could not do something about the weather. My secret was out!

We arrived off Tilbury where we transferred to small boats and were landed ashore. For security reasons, passengers were not allowed up the Thames. I phoned my sister Jane, giving her a surprise as she thought I was still in South Africa, and then made my way to her home in Surbiton; once there I phoned my parents in Gourock to let them know I had arrived. My father did not understand at first as I had left letters in Cape Town which my brother-in-law had posted at intervals – this ruse had managed to keep them all in the dark and had saved them from worrying. It was lovely to be home to experience an English winter after the heat and dust of South Africa. Snow had fallen and there had been a severe blizzard on the railway at Beattock causing a train to be stuck in a snowdrift. This delayed travel for many days on the west coast main line. The delay gave Jane and myself some time to catch up on all the news so the time was not entirely wasted. After some days I finally managed to travel North by the east coast main line, amply supplied with food by my side just in case of further disaster.

It was wonderful to be home again in Gourock; the snow was such that my brother George skied on the golf course.

As I said before, my father had already retired before the war, and he and my mother had moved north from Blackheath to Gourock in search of a house, letting out the Blackheath house to an army officer. Initially they rented a house in Ashton on the shores of the Clyde, then bought what they considered to be an ideal house in Tower Drive that would become the family home once extensive repairs were carried out before the move. From this new house my father would have a grand view of his beloved Clyde and as a dear friend lived across the water they would be able to communicate by telephone and telescope. In those days a call was not timed. At about the same time there was a need for a naval architect to supervise the construction of small boats in Dumbarton. Of course my father volunteered, but as he was over 65 by that time he could not be insured, so he ended up with an Air Raid Warden's job in Gourock instead.

After a few weeks I went back to Barts, my old hospital. I was ready to roll up my sleeves and nurse patients but was vexed to find that I was to work in the Home Department that looked after the student nurses. My duties consisted of checking in the nurses, meals, and weighing out some stores for the sisters and nurses in the wards.

Several evenings a week, volunteers came in to help us. On one occasion we were making quantities of butter pats to put on the tables. Each nurse was allowed two pats. One delightful helper remarked that she was very vexed she was not fit for the army, but she could tell any future grandchildren she made butterballs for Barts.

Miss Baines, our Assistant Matron, was very attractive and must have been beautiful when young. Miss Irvine, the Home Sister, was very strict, with a deep voice. Many nurses were rather afraid of her, but I always had admired her. She was very particular about our aprons that had to be kept meticulous.

By this time, German bombing raids were hitting London. When we had air raid warnings during the night it was my duty to see that all those on the register were present.

We were, of course, just in pyjamas, but somehow Miss Baines and Miss Irvine were always immaculate in their uniforms with little bows under their chins. They were so concerned for me and hoped I was able to sleep because the previous nurse had had a breakdown. I assured them that would not happen.

On one occasion, while my mother was down to make arrangements for the removal of the furniture from the house in Blackheath to Gourock, her new home now being ready for habitation, Miss Irvine insisted that I have a weekend off. I had great plans for a stay at a hotel in Kent where I was going to do quite a bit of riding. But it coincided with the evacuation at Dunkirk. All leave was cancelled and we were put on standby to receive possible casualties.

2

Queen Alexandria's Imperial Military Nursing Service and Ninth Casualty Clearing Station

During my time at St Bartholomew's, Miss Baines our Assistant Matron and Miss Irvine the Home Sister suggested that I should consider joining up with the Regulars in the Queen Alexandria's Imperial Military Nursing Service as a Reserve (Q.A.I.M.N.S.(R.)), although the Matron, Miss Dey, thought that my place was at St Barts, as I was also a midwife, and that I could spend the War in Families. However, they insisted that I should apply. Miss Jones the Matron-in-Chief of the Q.A.I.M.N.S. was a Barts trained nurse and had been one of their special students. I applied to the War Office to join the Q.A.I.M.N.S. Reserves. To my amazement I was called to the War Office for an interview. An elderly titled lady welcomed me and said, "Of course you have always wanted to join the Army," to which I replied, "No, this is only for the duration." When my Matron, Miss Dey, who was also part of the committee in the War Office, made the remark about me being a midwife, Miss Jones the Matron-in-Chief said, "Of course you know all about training orderlies."

When I replied in the negative she told me, "Of course you do, it's just the same as training probationers." At that I was thanked for attending the meeting.

I returned to St Barts and told my colleagues of my interview and that I did not expect to hear any more. I was amazed to receive a letter telling me that I had been accepted as a Reserve Regular and to report to Cambridge Hospital on 1 September 1940 where I would receive the necessary training to allow me to transfer to the Regulars at the end of the war. A travel warrant would be sent in due course. So that is how I started on the path that eventually sent me to India with all the adventures that were to go with it.

On 1 September 1940 I boarded a train for Aldershot as the sirens sounded. That was the first big blitz on London, but we had no alarms during my year in Aldershot.

Three of us were Reserve Regulars who were to be given the necessary training for the Regulars. The Colonel and Matron had returned from retirement to take charge of the hospital, which was well run, but some of the routines were very amusing. Each week there was an inspection, which was a complete charade, helped by having a veranda at the end of several of the wards, which opened on to a drive.

The sergeant of my ward told me that he would deal with everything. The table was filled with equipment that I had never seen. Inspection completed, it was the turn of the patients, those mobile at attention beside their beds and those in bed as near as possible to attention; then with thanks and a salute from the

Colonel the inspection team departed to the next ward. All the equipment was collected and taken out by the veranda and by the path and into the veranda of ward three, and set up ready for inspection. The Matron and Colonel were aware of the way the inspection was arranged and on one occasion the Colonel remarked, "I think that we have seen this floral arrangement already today."

During our stay at the Cambridge Hospital the Canadians came over and were stationed in the vicinity. The Canadian Sisters were paid far more than we and were commissioned officers. This resulted in a modest rise in pay for us from our £90 per annum and we were also 'commissioned' at the same time. Our kindly Colonel remarked, "I look on it as a privilege to salute my Sisters, but I suppose now you should salute me."

It was a very busy hospital and I had the accident and orthopaedic ward, mostly fractures with motorcycle despatch riders driving in the blackout; in those days fractures took a long time to be cured. They were a cheerful crowd – one was a school teacher who was embroidering a tablecloth for his wife. He had a severe fractured femur fixed with steel pins and resting on a Thomas splint. Tension was applied with weights attached to cords; this allowed the patient to move his position. It was important to prevent foot drop. I met a girl who was making equipment for hospitals in Scotland and asked her to make me a soft leather boot with laces and a loop on top. With a cord and a weight attached it was a great success and it supported his foot at all times. What advances have been made since then?

Another fellow called Bisics, who had a badly fractured leg, was a real rascal. On my first day, after the beds were made, he asked to borrow my scissors: my pockets were empty; he had pinched them; we all had a good laugh. He was the most cheerful Cockney with a heart of gold. The Red Cross was teaching him to make rugs and before moving to a convalescent hospital he offered to make one for me; it was very special and now adorns my grandson's bedroom floor.

We made several trips to London to order our uniform – what devastation after the blitz!

Three of us were Reserve Regulars and when our year was up we were posted. One, a very experienced Theatre Sister from the Glasgow Royal Infirmary, was posted to the Middle East, and Con Turner from St Thomas's and I from St Barts were posted to the Ninth Casualty Clearing Station (C.C.S.) at Knightshays Court in Tiverton. Our Unit consisted of a Regular-in-Charge who had already served a tour in India and eight Sisters, two of whom were much older than the rest of us. The 9th C.C.S was a Territorial Unit; the Sisters were the last to arrive. The medical officers had established themselves in the best rooms and we were given the servants' quarters, all behind baize-lined doors.

This was September, but later we had a very severe winter with several feet of snow; then they were all happy to be invited to our cosy sitting room with a coal fire. Our Colonel did not want to have Sisters but the rest were quite pleased with the arrangements.

We were busy training many new recruits, some very raw. I had one who came straight from coal-carrying duties to my training class; I asked him to request time to change into clean clothes before making an appearance in my classroom again. He had been a porter in a meat market in Glasgow and became an enthusiastic pupil and later in India a good nurse, looking after two Sisters in the officer's ward. His name was Todd.

We had final embarkation leave, and on 16 March 1942 we set off at night in total silence. We walked along a railway track avoiding the station, the reason being that troop movements were a secret. In the morning we were in Liverpool and embarked on a Dutch troopship S.S. *Johan van Oldenbarnavelt*. An R.A.F. officer was the C.O. for troops and R.A.F., the latter mostly having fought in the Battle of Britain. They were looking for female entertainment and we soon had our list of no-go areas. No-one would say where we were going except that large equipment was labelled Karachi. We set sail and in the morning we were anchored in Rothesay. We had to wait to be taken through the anti-submarine boom and then we anchored off Gourock … opposite my home!

A large convoy assembled and after about a week we sailed at night. We settled into our cabins, the eight of us together and our Sister-in-charge, Miss Meade, and a Matron who was to be the Principal Matron for India, Miss Wilkinson; she was a most charming and friendly person. There were eight R.A.F. Sisters in a nearby cabin.

Some days later we had engine trouble and were left behind by the convoy. A destroyer came to see if we were all right and kept in touch. We did not seem concerned; I think as we were young it was all an adventure. When repairs were completed we went full speed to catch up with the other ships. As we reached South Africa our half of the convoy was ordered to Cape Town. That was grand for me as my sister Mary was there and I had a few days with her and the children.

Troops were sent to Madagascar and after a time had to retreat, although while there they picked up a very virulent type of malaria. There was not even a supply of quinine, resulting in fatalities and also trailing this variety of the disease all across India.

The authorities knew when we were in Tiverton that we were going to the tropics though at the beginning we were not at war with Japan. We should have had training in tropical medicine and been supplied with the necessary drugs. We were at sea for six weeks with few duties and could have been studying Hindustani if we had been told that we were going to India.

3

India

We landed in Bombay on 16 May 1942 and two days later, after some rest, we set off on a busy train. After an endurance trip the Sisters were put off at Ahmadnagar, having travelled for some hours in considerable heat, and were taken to an Indian Military Hospital where we were to help out for a month before travelling on to our C.C.S. at Ranchi.

The hospital made us most welcome and invited us to come to dinner as soon as we were ready. The Matron was in formal evening uniform and the Voluntary Aid Detachment Nurses (V.A.D.s) were wearing gorgeous saris and obviously were from wealthy families. The meal was much enjoyed and served by bearers in magnificent uniforms. With many thanks we retired to our beds

It was an Indian military hospital and the next day we were shown round. The number of patients was far beyond its size, and huts had been added with earth floors. The patients were mostly British and from the later call-ups. They were being route marched in the heat of the day and suffering, some with heat stroke and others with malaria and dysentery. We soon learnt the treatment of tropical diseases, which proved very useful later.

To speak Hindustani became a necessity, particularly phrases such as to clean, to hurry, tea, water and the statement or question "all right(?)". We worked hard, but there was plenty of social life. The officers in a territorial unit from Calcutta invited us to dances and to play tennis. I asked if there was a chance of riding and if there was a horse, but the owner was on leave. A telegram was sent, and next day a Sikh arrived at my door early in the morning with the most beautiful horse called Flika, and away I went cantering over the plain and singing at the top of my voice to my horse. I went out riding either early morning or in the evening when it was cool. We had expeditions to the town in various forms of horse drawn transport.

Orders came for us to rejoin our unit, and with many thanks for the warm hospitality we set off on a long train journey to Ranchi in Bihar north of Calcutta. We were in a school near the town that had been taken over. It was a large, rather rambling building with plumbing, but the fresh water was stored in two separate tanks, one for drinking and the other for washing. The water was carried in containers to the bathrooms and kitchen and dining rooms by Indian servants called beasties; cleaners were called sweepers, the lowest sort of person, but ours were all women and were so happy; most carried a baby on their backs wrapped in a shawl and were very contented.

We still had our own men from our unit but there were Indian army personnel for other duties, such as cooks: they were very good and used charcoal fires.

Part of the Sisters' equipment was a Beatrice stove, consisting of a cast iron base for the paraffin oil with a tin chimney and a cast iron top to hold a dixie, this being carried in a canvas kit bag. All this to boil water and to sterilise equipment. Months later I was trying to make tablet for a party on my stove, being watched by our cook with interest. Suddenly he could stand it no longer and seized the dixie and finished it speedily on the charcoal fire.

Having been issued with my equipment and uniform I visited a very dear old cousin who had been in the Q.A.s in the First War. When she saw my uniform she said, "My dear, it is all the same, except your mess dress does not have whalebone supports."

The Medical Officers were glad to see us as they were very busy and were in need of some help. They were all housed in bungalows and we were given a bell tent each. I was delighted: this was what we were equipped for and what I was used to when camping with the Girl Guides. My father had enjoyed choosing all my gear; everything was marked with his special printing. I had a great time putting everything in its place.

Years later most was used camping with the Guides, then the family, and some were passed on to grandchildren. The floors were covered with bricks, with a brick pathway to the bathroom tent and the folding tripod canvas wash hand basin. When I wanted a bath the tripod opened out, then a large canvas was attached, filled with water from a bucket at hand to bale over.

Our patients were all British, new from home, suffering from malaria, dysentery and some with heat stroke. We were very busy and our experience in Ahmadnagar was very useful; our medical colleagues were often glad of our help. The problem was the shortage of equipment and, worst of all, drugs. No antibiotics, only Epsom salts for dysentery. In Aldershot we were treating prisoners with emetine; out here we had no sheets, only horse blankets; nursing these men with high temperatures ... they looked like gorillas. We lost too many patients, but we relied on Josie, our older Nursing Sister from Aberdeen, whose advice was readily accepted by us all, including our Sister-in-Charge, Miss Meade.

Unexpectedly we had a visit from our Principal Matron, Miss Wilkinson, and how welcome she was to us. She was a small lady but went into action. First, she tackled the Colonel. Her Sisters must be moved out of tents at once and quarters found even if it meant his officers moving into tents; after all, it was the monsoon season and very wet At once accommodation was found in a building for us.

We entertained Miss Wilkinson to tea in our quarters and she wanted to hear all our news. We told her of the shortages we were experiencing and she promised that she would inform the authorities in Delhi. She was rather horrified at the state of our white uniforms, which were washed in the river. She told us to get the local dhobies to make us either grey or khaki dresses and slacks and perhaps a suitable head dress for going in and out of tents in wet weather. Later when we were able to visit Calcutta we went to the officers' shop to have khaki bush jackets made to measure. I added a rather smart khaki beret. Later, towards the end of the war, we met nurses newly out from home who were somewhat critical of our unusual uniform. At home they were in officers' khaki.

There was an American camp a short distance away where Chinese were being trained to drive and maintain large Diamond 'T' trucks. We were invited to several parties and the meals were in Chinese style, certainly different and rather exciting.

Unfortunately Josie developed dysentery and was warded in a room next to the officers' ward; there was a balcony with a pleasant view. I followed her with the same complaint, and I must say we were very well looked after by our other older Sister, Gladys Matthews. Our orderly, Todd, the coal carrier from my nursing class in Tiverton, was splendid.

The night staff had always been complaining about the number of rats but this had not been taken seriously. However, when the lights were out I saw a large rat sitting on my locker eating an apple. I shouted to Josie and to Todd who came running. The rat fled and Todd remarked that after all I was under a mosquito net. Next night traps were set and Todd was kept busy throwing the bodies over the balcony and resetting the traps. Gladys looked after us so well and insisted on giving us a blanket bath. What a wonderful experience. There should be more hands-on nursing today; perhaps aromatherapy has taken its place.

Josie went to Darjeeling on sick leave for two weeks and returned telling me what a wonderful time she had, and advised me to stay with the same lady, who had lived there all her life. After some delay I was declared fit and sent for four weeks' sick leave. I also chose to travel to Darjeeling.

4

My First Glimpse of the Himalayas

I travelled overnight in a crowded train, which was suffocating despite fans and an open window. In the early morning we arrived at Siliguri at the foot of the hills, feeling jaded to put it mildly. Looking round I saw the foothills rising up and up into the sky: we were approaching the Himalayas.

First breakfast and into the café and it was still rather warm, but there was a fan waving overhead; a small boy was lying on the floor on his back with his toe wound round the cord attached to the fan, all very effective and peaceful.

I boarded the train to climb up to Darjeeling at seven thousand feet. The train was built in Scotland many years ago but the performance was a credit to the builders. We were welcomed aboard by two cheerful Sherpas who offered tea or cool drinks at intervals, a perfect start to a holiday. The train zigzagged to and fro and at one point did a figure of eight through a tunnel. Two coolies squatted on platforms each side of the engine with a sack of sand, which they scattered on the rails to stop the wheels slipping.

We climbed through all the climate zones in the time of two or three hours from the hot plains through pine trees and banks of mountain flowers. There were no fences or embankments, and the train chugged its way through villages, whistling, with children waving and hens and dogs scattering. It was delightful. Finally we came to the summit at 7,500 feet – and what a view, a whole range of snow-covered peaks as far as the eye could see, shining like gold in the sunshine.

It was my first sight of the Himalayas and I have never forgotten it.

I had arrived at my destination, Ghoom, and was warmly welcomed to my new quarters by a very charming hostess. Ghoom is three miles above Darjeeling. Our hostess had lived there all her life and her father had been a missionary and had started the first school. The other resident was a French detective, who was very interesting, and the next day he took me sightseeing. We explored the area and wandered through tea gardens all the time with wonderful views. Another day we set off very early to climb Tiger Hill and watch the sun rising over Everest, which was very special. It was still early but my friend suggested that we should visit the famous cowsheds belonging to the well-known dairy, where an exhibition was shown of the special precautions for hygiene at the milking session. We made our way into the sheds, and to our amazement the cows were being milked by rather grubby milkmen and there was no sign of much cleanliness. When we made a remark to the one in charge he was surprised and said that the display was only in the afternoons!

Darjeeling is the seat of government in the hot weather and is a mix of European buildings and native dwellings and bazaars. Here one sees hill men from the neighbouring States of Nepal and Tibet with Sikkim in between. The women of these parts are really lovely with their dark skins but pink cheeks, and always decorated with silver jewellery containing jade, turquoise and coral.

After about ten days I felt that I had seen all the local sights and that I would like to do something else. I decided that I would hire a pony and spend two days riding to Kalimpong. I went to see the Army Officer to tell him of my plans and he told me that if I went to see Mr Kydd at the *Darjeeling Times* anything he arranged was in order. I was welcomed by the gentleman, a most dynamic character who had organised the Sherpas for the early Everest expeditions, and he wondered what interest I would find in Kalimpong. I had two weeks left, and before long I found that I was to set off with a tent as the dak bungalows were all booked. I would go for ten days to reach Sandakphu – 11,929 feet up on the Singalila Ridge bordering Nepal on the West and Sikkim on the East and which ran on to reach the Himalayan giant of Kanchenjunga. I would have the tent and the sirdar Kippi would be in charge and that included me, and I was assured that I would be in good hands. Kippi was in the habit of going with a lady who was secretary of the Himalayan Club, a delightful person whom I met later when I became a member. Endless stores were bought and looked after by Kippi.

I was to camp beside the dak bungalows which were situated on the top of a hill and all over Sikkim within about 14 miles distance of each other, adequate for a day's march. They are provided for government officials on business or for other travellers when not required for their official purpose. The accommodation consisted of a combined sitting and dining room and two bedrooms, all with basic furniture; washing and toilet facilities were also available. Cooking facilities were available in the kitchen with supplies of wood, also sleeping accommodation for the porters. By camping near the bungalow I could use the toilet facilities, and the porters would have access to the cooking facilities and their sleeping quarters.

The detective friend who saw me off spoke fluent Hindustani, so I was unaware of the comments made by the older porter. He didn't want to travel with the white memsahib who spoke very little Hindustani and did not have her accommodation in the dak bungalows. When he returned to the house he told our kind landlady not to strip my bed, as I would be back. However, I was blissfully unaware of the comments, and the expedition set off in good spirits.

We left on 12 November at 10.45 a.m. The weather was perfect; it was after the monsoon with the rains over. The path was downhill and rather rough. We had a break for a packed lunch and then on and upwards, a good steep climb, and we had reached the bungalow of Jorpokri at 4.00 p.m., a distance of 10 miles and at the height of 7,400 feet. Here we had a fine view of the snow-clad mountains.

Kippi showed me the facilities that I could use in the bungalow and then pitched my tent. I unpacked what I needed for the night and had a walk round about.

Shortly I heard American voices, and a girl on a pony and two men appeared, followed by several porters. Shortly after, a head popped into my tent and the owner introduced herself and asked me to join them for a meal in the bungalow. She was interested in my little tent, which held all my needs.

We had a delightful meal and exchanged stories of activities. They were missionaries in Burma but had to leave due to the war and they were now employed by the Americans. We found that we had several mutual friends. Before turning in we walked a little way and gazed at the fine view with the colours of the setting sun on the snow-covered mountains. With many thanks I said good night to these kind friends and crawled into my little tent with the entrance tied back and into my sleeping bag, and with this view I was soon fast asleep.

As I woke Kippi appeared with a big mug of hot tea, then after giving me time to get washed and dressed he served a fine cooked breakfast. By 8.00 a.m. we were packed and away, our next bungalow Tonglu a distance of 10 miles.

We followed a rough path down and over a small bridge and then by a zigzag path up a steep hill. We stopped at a little busti, a small collection of little houses or shacks. Evidently old friends, and we had a warm welcome. Kippi obviously explained about his charge and insisted on finding a small stool for me to sit on. This was a very special experience: I was now one of the family.

A lovely young girl was sitting on the ground and bathing her small baby in a saucepan. I was able to talk to her and took a photo. The rest of the family came out and greeted me, and the mother came and took me by the hand and gave me her rosary, which I did my best to refuse as it was so special; however, she insisted by putting it between my hands and holding them together, which was accompanied with her blessing. At this point I had no option but to thank her as best I could in her own language. To this day I still have this as a very special treasure.

Fond farewells and we were off again up a steep path till we reached our next bungalow of Tonglu at 10,774 feet, and what a view, the whole range of the Kanchenjunga group as well as the Chola range that marks the boundary of Sikkim, the white peaks of Chumolhari (24,000 ft.) overlooking Bhutan and beyond to Tibet.

Before pitching my tent Kippi made his welcome cup of tea and I sat and just enjoyed the beauty of my surroundings. Again there was a fine meal of soup and chicken with plenty of vegetables, ending with bread and cheese and coffee. As the sun set the colours on the snows changed gradually from gold to pink and finally to a sort of silver as the moon came up. By now I was ready for my sleeping bag and another sound sleep.

Next morning I was awake and the whole view was pure gold on the snows from East to West. Kippi's cheerful face appeared and the mug of tea – up and dressed, breakfast, packing and off at 9.00 a.m. We had a big day ahead of us: 14 miles.

The path was fairly good but with many ups and downs and always steeper, then suddenly we saw the triple crest of Sandakphu – our goal, but still some heavy marching, mostly through bamboo glades, and still climbing. Then suddenly a small clearing and a pool with the name Kalapokri meaning black pool. It was the ideal place for lunch. We still had five miles to go.

After some more steep and rough climbing, we had reached our destination, and what a panorama! It was four o'clock and daylight, I was standing on the Singalila Ridge looking due North at the whole horizon of snow clad mountains, in the West Everest (29,002 ft) and on to Kanchenjunga (28,156 ft), then the whole range extending East across the horizon towards Tibet and Butan. This was the most wonderful view that I had ever experienced and will never forget. Mountaineers who have climbed all over the globe declare that there is no finer view than this in the world. What a privilege to have had this opportunity.

I was more than ready for the usual fine meal and made a point of thanking the Sherpas for the hard work of carrying their loads over such difficult tracks. The loads are carried on the back with webbing attached and held round their head. An early night was called for, and again the wonderful shade of pink on the snows.

Next morning I looked round and wondered what I might do. I gazed over towards Nepal and saw a hill that looked interesting. Kippi did not agree and talked about chitties; however, he saw that I was determined to go, so off we went and had a great time, but as usual in my family it took longer than expected, doing that little extra bit round the next corner!

It was dusk when we reached the bottom of the hill near our home. There was a man in uniform talking to Kippi, and I sat on a wall patiently waiting and quite unconcerned. Eventually my friend came along swinging a dead chicken and said that had been a frontier policeman, that I had no right to be in Nepal and that he should have arrested me. Kippi said that his good face and his Buddhist hat had saved the day. I must explain that Kippi was of a Lama family and so could wear this silk purple hat.

We started up the hill and it was by this time getting dark; to my horror figures were coming down the hill with hurricane lamps, blankets and stretchers. A traveller had arrived to be told that a rescue was needed. However, we kindly refused the help and returned unaided, though weary and glad to reach the bungalow.

Kippi was glad to accept the help of the other traveller's cook in providing a very delightful meal ending with mugs of hot, sweet tea. I told my version of my exciting day and no doubt Kippi had a different tale to tell. I was really tired and crawled into my sleeping bag and had a long sleep.

My fellow traveller worked with the railways and asked me if I would join him on his trip. Needless to say I declined, and anyhow he was going along the Singalila Ridge to Phalut, but I agreed to walk some of the way. Kippi came too, as he was determined to keep an eye on me after yesterday's experience. We turned back after a spell and then wandered along and sat down to have our lunch. When we were within sight of the bungalow I assured Kippi that I would not wander away, and I settled down at a good spot.

I just revelled in the scenery and thought about how so many famous mountaineers had described this view as the finest in the world in clear weather. I thought of Tom McKinnon, a very dear friend and also a climbing friend of my brother, and of Tom Weir and Douglas Scott, who were all members of The Scottish Mountaineering Club. They went on an expedition to Nepal in 1952, and later Tom was chosen for the attempt on Kanchenjunga; he was one of those who reached the summit. He would have walked along this ridge on his way.

I sat dreaming and just storing up memories of the views and all my surroundings and adventures and the fellowship with my Sherpa friends. Now sixty years later I am writing this on my computer in my lovely little flat in Greenock, and I remember every little detail as if it was yesterday.

We were in the middle of a war and I was only six months in the country, on sick leave and then fit and able to undertake this exciting trek and being accepted by these Sherpas as a friend. It had all happened with meeting Mr Kydd. What a fantastic character – he seemed to be sure that I would enjoy myself.

I was fortunate in not being affected by mountain sickness, which is caused by insufficient oxygen. It causes severe headaches and sickness and seems to be something to do with the individual's chemistry. I was unaware of the problem and had been living at 70,000 feet for two weeks, and on the trek we had moved gradually to increased heights. It seems to affect some individuals and not others, and I seem to have been one of the lucky ones.

The last evening we were able to use the sitting room, as there were no other travellers. The meal was always chicken, but Kippi seemed to have a variety of recipes. A last walk in the evening was spent watching the changing colours on the mountains before turning in.

It was 17 November and time to start back; we were all packed and ready and heading for Rimbick some seven miles away. The first part was returning the way we had come and was a rough scramble down and then after a stop for some refreshment we came to a small Buddhist monastery and I said that I would very much like to visit if that was possible.

My friends were delighted as they were Buddhists. An elderly priest came and greeted me. He had long white hair and a long beard and a very kind face. Bowing, he took hold of my hands, blessing me, and took me into the chapel and sat me down at the back. The Sherpas were delighted and went up to the altar and then a cheerful service followed with bells ringing, horns blowing and drums beating. They kept looking back to see if I was enjoying myself, then incantations which were their prayers and I was able to join in my own way. I felt that we were all praying for peace. The service ended and the Sherpas were giving the priest money, but he shook his head at me and brought out a special book written in English with a message from the Maharajah. I was expected to write a message and make a note of my donation. With another blessing and assurance that I would be added to the prayer flags, we said our farewells, and what very special memories I had to add to my story.

From Rimbick, with its forest bungalow at 7,500 feet, it was possible to see Darjeeling. From now on there were no other travellers in the bungalows, so my tent was packed away.

Next day we were heading for Jephi, a distance of eleven miles. It was a steep path about five miles down to a bridge and then through cultivated ground, winding round the mountainside, and Jephi was reached. At the height of 4,100 feet, we were returning to civilisation as there were some shops, but the bungalow was in a sheltered position and there were banks of lovely wild flowers.

We set off for Darjeeling, the paths going up and down. At one point on a spur there was a clear view of the town. Finally a steep path led for over five miles to a bazaar at the bottom of the town. Here were some British women nearby, and I was doing some shopping with advice from my Sherpa friends midst much laughter, and the looks aimed at me were of horror that I was fraternising with natives. I smiled at them but did not introduce myself as a British Nursing Officer. I must have looked like a gypsy, very sunburnt, hair somewhat ruffled and looking so happy and at home. It was sad that folk had to feel that they were so superior. Later I met a similar feeling towards the ordinary

British Tommy, that one could not invite them into one's drawing room – though they would gladly help in many other ways.

Our final walk was to the office of the *Darjeeling Times* and to Mr Kydd; he was delighted to see us. The Sherpas were paid, and I thanked them warmly and signed their books, the comments in the one for Kippi being very special; he had been on the early Everest expeditions. Kippi stayed, and Mr Kydd wanted to hear the whole story. He was horrified to learn of the visit into Nepal. No one was allowed over the border and it was a miracle that I had not been arrested and interned for the duration.

I tried to make excuses that he had not told me that I must not stray over the border. That brought forth a *torrent* of words. He said that he did not know me but that he would remember if I returned again. I assured him that he could expect a return visit whenever possible.

Mr Kydd was determined that I would end my holiday in style. He would arrange everything, and I was to be at the Ghoom station in time for the mail train next evening.

I had been invited to stay at the Sister's Mess, so Kippi took me and all my luggage and assured me that he would fetch me in good time. I was made so welcome; we had a most delicious meal and it was good that chicken was not on the menu. I was thoroughly spoilt and revelled in a hot bath, a long sleep in a most comfortable bed, and breakfast brought to me in bed. It was good to exchange news. The staff were older and had been posted to have lighter duties and to be in cooler weather.

Kippi arrived on time and introduced his wife who gave me a gift of eggs – and what a beautiful young lady! She carried most of my luggage, and we set off to meet Mr Kydd. I said my goodbyes and climbed into my vehicle, which was a trolley on wheels, running on the rails. The seats were well upholstered and I sat in style in the back with my luggage and the driver, a magnificent vision in Victorian uniform having a brake and a horn. With a push and a cheer from my friends we set off down the mountainside. What a thrill rushing down with horn blowing, children waving and cheering. All down through the grand scenery and then we were at the bottom. The Calcutta train had to wait and hook us on to take us to the station. My kind driver took me and my belongings to my carriage. We parted with very many thanks for a fantastic trip.

There were three ladies sharing the compartment who welcomed me with amazement, witnessing my trip. They were teachers who had visited Darjeeling several times and had no idea that such a trip was available, and there was I, only having been in the country for a short time, having all these adventures. We had a pleasant meal on the train and settled down for the night. Next morning, through Calcutta, off to Ranchi and I had a warm welcome from my friends who were eager to hear about my leave and were amazed to see me looking so well.

It was good to be back, and I was eager to get on with the job of nursing our troops.

5

Chittagong

A new Colonel was posted to the unit and we were delighted. The war was moving down the Arakan peninsula and we were under orders to be ready to move to Chittagong. On 3 January 1943 we started on a most memorable and fascinating journey.

We were dressed in khaki slacks and scarves tied over our heads. We had packed all the necessary belongings for several days. It was night time and the roads were very dusty. After a couple of hours we arrived at a station and settled in with the help of our very faithful batman. We dosed off and on and next arrived at the Bramaputra River. Here we embarked on a river steamer, sank into bunks and slept while others shifted all the gear. Refreshed next morning, we enjoyed the sail to our next port and boarded another train, which would take us to our final destination. We had the whole train and the Sisters were in the end coach. We stopped for lunch with tea made with boiling water from the engine, and our batman brought it to us along with ship's biscuits and a tin of Libby's corn beef each, so at the end of the journey we had quite a stock. We went at a very modest pace and it was fascinating to sit and gaze at the country and the people. Children came running to us offering oranges, which we gladly bought to quench our thirst in the heat, and thought of folks at home who had no such luxuries. Our dinner was either cooked at the rail side, usually stew; or if we were near a suitable station, dinner would be ordered and we would sit down and really enjoy our meal.

Next day we steamed into Chittagong and were met by our old Colonel; however, we were welcomed very warmly at the hospital by the senior surgeon and physician, both of Major rank.

This was an Indian hospital for one hundred patients and they had one thousand; they were desperate for trained staff. Needless to say we were thankful at last to have arrived at a place where we were needed.

We had a very pleasant unfurnished bungalow on a hill with a rambling garden, a water supply, full plumbing and a bathroom with a bath – what luxury. With the unpacking done we were shown round the hospital. The main building was being used for the most serious surgical cases with an officers ward upstairs. The most serious medical patients, who were all Indian, were on stretchers in a marquee on the front lawn.

Round the side were huts made of wattle, straw and with wooden supports, called bashers; the mobile surgical patients were accommodated there. The medical walking, mostly recovering from dysentery and malaria, were in tents on a slope just with a ground sheet and a blanket; they had to collect their food and medicines.

Our bungalow was pleasant and we managed with our camp furniture. The garden, though overgrown, was full of interesting plants, including pineapples. One of our Sisters developed chicken pox and was isolated in a tent on our front lawn.

We were by the railway, which went down the peninsula to Cox's Bazaar, where the 14th Army were fighting, so the casualties came to us by train. Our Sister in charge gave us all our areas of work; we were very busy and worked well as a team. We faced the same old problem as before: shortages, this time especially of stretchers and basic needs for the men who probably had been separated from their small kit – shaving, eating, cooking utensils and the like.

I had the surgical ward with theatre, sharing the work with other Sisters. One day when we had a trainload in from the front it included two Japanese, obviously officers of high rank. They were fairly badly wounded and needed treatment under anaesthetic. One stoutly refused; they had obviously been told that they would be mutilated and then killed. He was taken to the theatre, and I will never forget the awful struggle and the look of terror on his face. Surgery completed, he was returned to his bed, and his expression when he came round was special. Perhaps he had a story to tell after the war, when he returned to Japan.

When I was in the medical ward in the marquee on the beautiful front lawn I asked the Major if it would be a good idea to send the stretchers down to the tents, as ground sheets were adequate in the marquee. Leaving instructions to our staff, we went for lunch. On returning, to my horror, I met the Colonel in the process of supervising my orderlies carrying the stretchers back to the lawn. I asked, "Were these your instructions?" and when he answered, "Yes," I was very angry. I am afraid that I replied extremely rudely, saying he "should be in charge of a prison camp, not a hospital". I supposed that I might have been severely disciplined and sent home in disgrace. However, two years later when I was on the hospital ship he came on board and met me when he was with our Colonel, greeted me kindly, and remarked, "I see that you have one of our 9th C.C.S. Sisters, wonderful women." Perhaps I had done him some good.

For a period, General Wavell took over in India and his wife was with him. She decided to visit us and we were delighted as, after all, we expected that she would have tea with us. We felt that even though the Colonel would be with us, whoever was lucky enough to sit beside her must tell her of the shortages. She first inspected the hospital and caused concern by diving into the kitchen unexpectedly and making some criticisms.

Our cook excelled himself with his baking. She was charming and so interested in all that we were doing and promised that she would take action. She told the Colonel that she would send one of her assistants to visit and assess what were our requirements.

The visit was made soon afterwards, and, would you believe it, all the small kits for the men were found in the storeroom. So our casualties were given a set of pyjamas, a towel and all toilet needs; more supplies would be delivered, including stretchers.

Meanwhile the troops were fighting in appalling conditions in the jungle with inadequate equipment. It was constant advance and retreat. The British Tommy is the finest in the world, grumbling away but with a cheerful grin and just making the best of things, always ready to lend a helping hand to anyone in need. The casualties came up from Cox's Bazaar by train, the very serious being flown to specialist hospitals.

When I was on night duty it was rather hectic. I had a British sergeant and the rest were Indian nursing orderlies. Those needing special care were within easy reach. On a round of the other patients usually there were few problems, but some instinct would alert you, and you would find there was someone needing rather urgent attention.

One night we were notified of a load of casualties arriving and the rather new officer thought that we should call the day staff, but I persuaded him to wait and see. The main surgical patients were in the building, so I put on the lights and asked all those who were mobile to gather their belongings together and to find a bunk in the basher huts. There was no question of changing sheets.

The train duly arrived with a large number of badly injured cases, most on stretchers and those with leg injuries in Thomas splints, which consisted of a padded ring which fitted into the groin with the leg supported on a pad and attached to a metal rod extending beyond the foot, then firmly secured to the stretcher, so if there was a fracture tension could be applied.

In these circumstances beds were not needed, and the men were happily settled on the veranda. The day surgical team were very thankful that they had not been called out, as we were very short staffed. .

The next evening when I was on my rounds one young officer who had lost his right arm said, "Never mind, we did our best and what we were asked." Later that evening Churchill broadcast and told of the progress that had been made on the European front, and announced, "Then we will make a move in India." Hearing those words left us all shattered and I am sure lost him his election after the war.

Constantly advances were ordered and made before the necessary equipment was in place, causing retreat and heavy casualties. It was just the same with us: apply to Delhi and have a reply in several months.

In August 1943 South East Asia Command was formed under Lord Louis Mountbatten, and in October General William Slim was made Commander of the 14th army.

When it was announced that Mountbatten was taking charge, the idea that he was a sailor was something the troops were not happy about. However, when he arrived in Chittagong the troops were drawn up in formation. He then said to them, "Gather round," and asked for a soapbox. First he told them how things were at home, and then he made them a promise: "There will be no advance until the equipment is in your hands," and that really boosted the morale – he dispensed with red tape, with good results.

I was posted to Calcutta to take a theatre course and went on the troopship S.S. *Melchior Treub,* which took our casualties to Calcutta with a medical and nursing team from the S.S. *Wusueh*. The reason the *Wusueh* team were also on board was that the *Wusueh* was not suitable for the task during the monsoon season as a result of the weather. When I left the ship the Colonel made remarks about the amount of luggage that I had for one who was in a mobile unit (I had added a tin trunk for a gramophone and records). I reported at the army hospital and was made welcome. During an enjoyable supper I was talking to three Sisters, who remarked that they were on night duty. When I asked them how many patients they had, the reply was three hundred. I told them that I had just come off nights and had 1,000 patients with a trained sergeant and some Indian nursing orderlies. No wonder that we were called the Forgotten Army.

I thoroughly enjoyed the course and the company and returned to Chittagong, this time by train, riverboat and train again. I was the only woman travelling, and at the last stage I was sitting on my trunk waiting for someone to find my 'ladies only' compartment

A Chinese officer came up and said that I was the Sister who had looked after him in Chittagong and he set off to find my carriage, turned out the occupants, and settled me in with my luggage and left me with a charming smile and a smart salute.

It was good to be back with all my friends. We were a very happy team and worked well together, backing each other up. We caught up with leave and a big event: one Sister got married to an officer we all knew in Ranchi. The wedding dress was made and the party was in the bungalow and garden with a padre performing the ceremony and our surgeon giving away the bride.

There was a mixed British and Indian artillery unit in the area, and the officers invited us to various social events. I asked if there would be a chance of some riding. This was easy, as they were a cavalry unit

Miss Meade, our Sister-in-charge, was very pleased to join the other officers, the countryside was very suitable, and for me this was a special way to relax and forget problems, be able to canter along just talking to my horse.

Later we had a visit from our Principal Matron, Miss Wilkinson, as the unit was to move down towards the front line, but after the deaths and treatment of some of her Sisters she had decided that we were to be replaced with extra men. This was what our unit had been trained for; we had been working hard, but we had had decent living conditions and had never been in any danger, and now we were not to take our place with the men in our unit. Regretfully, we accepted her decision.

The Sisters were all to be posted to other units and I was asked if I was still keen to serve on a hospital ship. Needless to say I was absolutely delighted, and my orders were to join hospital ship *Melchior Treub*. Little did I know how my life was to change as the result of being welcomed aboard by Chief Officer Soep.

Many years later I realised that our Principal Matron, Miss Wilkinson, knew that there was a trooper being converted to a hospital ship, so this was why she had sent me on the theatre course, knowing that a theatre Sister would be required. How grateful I am, but I only wish that I had contacted her to tell her of the result of her kindly thought.

Sixty years later I was asked to become a member of the Burma Star Association and have learned of the heroic work performed by Q.A.s up at the front line at the battles of Imphal and Kohima.

When you go home,
Tell them of us and say,
For their tomorrow,
We gave our today.

The Kohima Epitaph

Now I must introduce Bernard.

6

Introduction to Bernard Soep

Bernard Soep was born on 1 September 1904, in Amsterdam. His mother Sophie, who had cause to leave her husband when Bernard was only a toddler, brought him up along with his older brother. She took them with her bicycle from Antwerp to Amsterdam where Asher's, the diamond cutters, took her on. When she was sufficiently proficient she was given the task of polishing some of the small diamonds of the famous Koh-i-Nor diamond stone, which had been presented to King Edward VII by South Africa. This gem was so precious that very elaborate precautions were taken with a special ship and a special safe. In the end, first class post was used and it arrived safely. Sophie would bring her workpieces home in her handbag and polish them on a machine, rather like a treadle sewing machine. The boys were allowed to watch but not touch.

Bernard was allowed to join in the May Day parade to walk beside the big drum and carry the red flag. Sophie was the first woman to be in the Dutch parliament.

Later his brother Leo went back to his father, but Bernard was very close to his mother. He was determined to go to sea and so ran away for six days. He had some rather dangerous adventures and on return his mother decided to encourage him to get into Nautical School. Here he enjoyed the studies, served as a Cadet and passed his Third Mate's exam in 1926. After this he entered service with the K.P.M. Dutch Packet Company based in Batavia, running ships in the Far East. He gained his further qualifications in Batavia, ending with his Master's Ticket finally in 1933. Promotion was in strict order and it was January 1937 before he was appointed as a Chief Officer.

In October 1942, Bernard was appointed as Chief Officer of S.S. *Melchior Treub*, which was taken over as a troopship. In December 1943 she was converted in Garden Reach workshops, India, into Hospital Ship Number 6.

Bernard had amazing adventures during his service in the Far East. He kept a diary and later he wrote the stories for the *Nautical Magazine*. In February 1946 he resigned, as he had been told that I should not return to the tropics, since I had suffered repeated attacks of amoebic dysentery as well as a mild dose of cholera.

In 1936, when he was on leave, he had a very special holiday with his mother, expecting to see her next time, but war broke out in Europe. Leo, Bernard's brother, invited his mother to come and stay with his family near the Spanish border, which might be safer, but she said that she had a job to do in Amsterdam. She joined the underground movement as she spoke fluent French, German, Spanish and English and she would be able to help allied troops to escape. She did great work but later she was arrested and the fact that she was also

Jewish born did not help. She was imprisoned in Auschwitz, where she died ... Bernard was devastated.

A very brave and remarkable woman, and I am proud to be her daughter in law. One granddaughter bears her name.

Now that you know a little about Bernard, here is the first of several stories of his exploits, which are reprinted (with slight modifications) with the kind permission of the *Nautical Magazine*.

7

Treason on the High Sea

By Captain Bernard Soep

This was first published as an article in the Nautical Magazine, *Vol. 242, No. 6, December 1989, and appears here by courtesy of the Editor.*

"Doea mata sapi" (literally "cows'eyes") – "Two fried eggs," I told the djongos who took my order for breakfast, "and lots of coffee." I felt content, sitting in the dining room of the Company hotel in Batavia. This was the start of a two week holiday and I planned to take the train to Bandoeng that same afternoon and stay there as base for climbing the neighbouring tops of which there are three or four of over 3,000 metres. But it was not to be; I was sipping my second coffee, when I was handed a slip from the manager: "Please phone Mr Williams" (our Marine Superintendent), and my spirits plunged ... I had left my ship only last night ... and the phone call confirmed my forebodings ... to join the *Kalimati* that very day ... at my convenience. The Chief Officer had been hospitalised with acute appendicitis ... and the ship was due to sail tomorrow morning at 8 am ...

Instead of blowing my top, I was rather pleased; the *Kalimati* was our largest cargoship of 9,000 tons and due to sail for South Africa, etc., with a general cargo. For the previous eight months, I had been on a 2,000-ton passengership, ferrying between Botavia and Pontianak twice weekly, and could look forward to some real navigation and ... lovely climate, quite a change from the tropical humid weather at the start of the monsoon in February 1940, in this part of the world.

And though the war had so far been restricted to Western Europe and mostly a 'Propaganda War' at that with the dropping of leaflets, it was clear that this would not last much longer, proved by the increased activities at sea by a huge fleet of U-boats and the knowledge that German pocket battleships were roaming at will on the seven seas, not respecting any neutral shipping. The small countries, like the three in Scandinavia, Holland and Belgium, thought that a strict neutrality could help them to stay out, that is what they hoped anyway ... and orders had gone out to paint the national colours on the sides of all neutral ships to tell the U-boat commanders we were just innocent bystanders ... and I wanted to be more actively involved in this struggle against Germany and its madman Hitler.

I joined the ship that afternoon at 6.00 p.m. She showed all the signs of being ready for sea; hatches closed and secured with kegs, derricks lowered and shipshape.

The *Kalimati* had been built in Hamburg in 1928 and been purchased in 1932, when our company had embarked on a major expansion programme. Over a five-year period, 16 ships had been added to our fleet of 110 ships either newly built or purchased second hand, the majority being less than 3,000-tons, mixed cargo-passengerships, specially suited for the inter-island-service of the then Dutch East Indian Archipelago of over 2,000 islands, but also six purely cargoships of over 6,000-tons of which the *Kalimati* was the largest at 9,000-tons. It was anticipated that our scope would be expanded to China, the Philippines, India, and South Africa; we already had regular services with Australia. And last but not least, daily services with Singapore. The intake in staff, however, had not kept pace with the numbers of officers and experienced masters available in Holland.

There were two main reasons for that. Though the pool of seafaring men was large enough, in those days, the tropics still had a bad name for health reasons; to sign a contract for four years at a time was not very attractive either. So it came about that they looked abroad, especially to Germany, where there was a huge number of ex-navy people, now that the war-fleet had ceased to exist.

A dozen ex-U-boat officers had been engaged, of which now only three were still in the company, and one of those was my future master.

The second officer, Hobbema was his name, took me to the captain's cabin and introduced me. When we came in, he was standing in the middle of his cabin. He was of normal height, a slim good figure, well-shaven, close cropped light-brown hair and light-blue eyes.

He did not shake hands, but said: "Glad to have you with us, the second officer can give you all the information you require," and picking up a large roll of paper from his table, "Here is the cargo plan, as Mr Hamer took ill, the last couple of days."

And with these words he turned his back on us and sat down; clearly the interview was over, and we left...

"Well", said Hobbema, "You won't be surprised to learn that he is a member of the N.S.B." (the equivalent in Holland of the Nazis and the New Fascist Party of Mosley in Great Britain). "That should not make any difference with his job as Ship's Master," I said ... and sincerely hoped so ... "Our departure has been set at 8 a. m. as the mail will arrive at 7," Hobbema said. "You want to be shown round before dinner at 7.30 or rather tomorrow?"– "No, that's fine, now will do."

The *Kalimati* had the funnel and engineroom, aft, the crew's quarters and mess, toilets and washrooms and the large galley. Also the two cabins for the four tally-clerks and a little office. These were all on the main deck. On the deck above were two lifeboats, one on either side of the engine-room skylight (it crossed my mind, that they were an awful long way from our cabins ...) To round this off, a large steering house on the poop with the quadrant; above that, a small deck with the handsteering gear and a binnacle with compass.

The bridgehouse, which had four decks, was roughly in the centre of the ship, with two holds forward and three aft. A large saloon plus pantry on the main deck, above that, cabins for all officers, toilets and

bathrooms, the whole surrounded by a six-foot-wide
deck. Stairways on either side led to the bridgedeck
above.

The bridge proper was big, four large windows in
front of the binnacle and steering gear and behind that a
small chart room with a connecting door to the
captain's suite behind, (sittingroom, bedroom and
bathroom). The radio-station was in the back with a
bed-sitting room for Sparks, which led outside to the
deck. A small deck above the bridge, called the
monkeydeck, complete with compass, finishes this
description.

At dinner that night I met the chief engineer and two
of the other five, and all three deck-officers besides
myself. The two absent engineers were married and
spent their last night at home. From deck, funnily
enough, none were married, except the captain, but his
wife lived in Bandoeng, I was told.

The captain was conspicuous by his absence. 'Chief'
told me: "He always has all his meals in his cabin. All
communication with me is done by telephone or by
short notes." The second engineer, Koopman was his
name, chipped in: "I have been on board with him for
over a year and as far as I remember, he has spoken to
me once, and I can't even remember about what." He
continued: "You'll find, that as far as you are
concerned, he is an ideal captain, he never interferes,
unless he is quite sure something is amiss. Every day,
he goes round, never at the same time, a notebook in
his hand, does not ask any questions, just looks. He had
your predecessor in his cabin on several occasions, but

we never knew what it was about, but Hamer always called the Serang immediately after ..."

"Except for the navigation," said Hobbema, "all courses are pencilled in the charts with added notes ... 'Call me here' ... but then again, he never takes an observation, and I doubt whether he has a sextant; we have not seen it." Sparks added his contribution: "His one and only hobby seems to be his radio; he has a magnificent Philips set, which is on almost continuously, day and night; here Hobbema can tell you, on his watch from midnight till 4.00 a.m., he can see our master listening intently and making notes, his door is never shut," and Hobbema again: "No second guess of what he is listening to, the thumping 'umpahs' of the Horst Wessel march are clearly audible ..."

After dinner, I retired to my cabin, a nice roomy one, doubled up as office, complete with a desk and safe. It had a proper window, not a porthole. Then smoking my pipe, I felt content and reflected on the day's events; that meeting with captain Bauer, it occurred to me that we had not exchanged names ... probably due to the fact that he did not take my outstretched hand ... He knew mine of course, from the letter of posting, and head office had told me his name ... it was rather off-beat ... odd ...

But there was nothing odd about the cargoplan he had made, that was a work of art; of size 1 metre x 25 centimetres, it gave a full outline of the holds with all consignments in colour of destination and inked-in markings, drawn in their exact locations in the holds. On the side was a legend of their destination-colours and I learnt that our itinerary was, in sequence: Rodriguez, Mauritius, Reunion, Beira, Laurenco Marquez, Durban, East London, Port Elizabeth, Mosselbay, Capetown.

I was in the chartroom at 6 o'clock, to get an idea of distances and time involved. The first stretch to Rodriguez was 2,920 miles, about 11 days at our maximum speed of 10 knots and we could be in Capetown in the first week of March.

The mail arrived in due time, 112 bags which we stored in the strong room, and we sailed on the dot of eight; by midnight we cleared Str. Sunda into the Indian Ocean.

The weather was fine, the atmosphere on board very pleasant, added to which, the long moderate high ocean swell from the S. W. produced a languid, lazy holiday feeling by the regular rolling and pitching movement of the ship. I was hardly aware of Captain Bauer's presence, meeting him regularly only once a day, at noon, when he came into the chartroom, binoculars slung round his neck, to check the noon's position, which I gave him and he then pencilled this in the chart, whereupon he walked several times round the bridge, not saying a thing ... this never varied and he vanished into his cabin after a few moments ... (very odd, we all thought). I also met him occasionally on one of his daily rounds of inspection, when he exchanged a few words like "Fine day, Mr Soep," from him and "So it is, captain," from me ... Once he called me to his cabin to ask me what we had for Rodriguez and I told him: two bags of mail for the British station of Cable and Wireless, the only occupants of the island.

Some 500 miles from Rodriguez, the weather deteriorated and we had a typhoon warning from St Louis, the capital of Mauritius; it would pass (the centre), 300 miles north of us. A high swell, heavy rain showers and a wind force 7/ 8 were the indications of it passing and by the time we dropped anchor at Rodriguez, all was peaceful once again.

We kept ourselves well-informed with the events in Europe. Besides the Master's radio-set, we had three more receivers on board, the Chief Engineer and the Third, both had one and our clerks had one, but the last one was very small and could not receive the B.B.C., our main source of information. I had an extremely good set ... a Philips with so-called 'magic eye', a green light which came on when the tuning was correct.

We shared our 'news', of course, of what we picked up; for instance, the storming of the *Altmark* in Norwegian waters, on the 16th February, had caused great excitement, especially when it was made known that the majority of the 300 freed men had been crews of ships torpedoed in the Indian Ocean. As a direct result I had doubled our 'look-outs' to two (one in the crow's-nest and one on the bow, to be changed every hour). I asked for volunteers, as we needed over a dozen men for that, and all three clerks came forward and the two 5th engineers.

Strangely enough, we had seen no traffic at all, but this changed after Rodriguez; we crossed the shipping along the African coast.

After Beira, going south, one would never have thought there was a war on: the whole coast, especially the towns, were fully lit and the passing ships about 10 miles off land must have been easy targets for the German U-boats at over 10 miles off.

We had left Mosselbay on the 2nd March at midnight and were on the last lap to Capetown. Little wind, perhaps force 1 / 2, it just rippled the ocean-surface, visibility was poor and the air was chilly and felt wet. When daylight came at 5.30, I was on watch. A mist bank covered the horizon from east through south to N.W.; the northern side was clear. At 5.50 the look-out in the crow's nest reported something on the port-side. I searched with my binoculars, but found nothing.

I sent a sailor up for some clarification and he came down with the look-out (one of the clerks), who told me that he saw some of the tops of a sailing ship sticking out of the mist ... "A large ship, sir, about there," and he pointed to about 30 degrees on the port-side. At that precise moment, as if on cue, a large four-masted barque emerged from the gloaming, shaking off the mist shroud that enveloped her, with a full spread of canvas from the main skysail on the maintop down to the flying jib on the end of the bowsprit, and all drawing a little from whatever breeze available ... "What a sight," beautiful does not describe it ... a fairytale image, I searched for words, a memory of the past. She seemed to have a more westerly course ... Her Morse-light called us and I replied KALIMATI, "Who is she?" asked the Captain's voice behind me. "I don't know, she only just appeared." ... "Oh, there it is!" I said when once again her signal came: PREUSSEN ... "Oh," said the Captain; he sounded agitated, excited. "I'll answer that," and I stepped aside. To my utter surprise he tapped in German: "NAMEN KAPITAN BITTE" ... at that moment, Ch.E. Jansen joined us and Jansen exclaimed: "That is a sight for sore eyes," not grasping what had just happened. What followed was sensational: the *Preussen* signalled a long dash, and ... altered course, away from us, leaving us utterly flabbergasted, then she disappeared once again, swallowed up by the mist ... We all looked at our master, who was actually swearing, in German (from excitement, I thought), "Donnerwetter" ... he looked perplexed, scanned the horizon once again with his glasses ... "A friend of yours, Captain?" ... asked Mr Jansen mischievously, I thought ... Captain Bauer looked at him ... "No" ... and left the bridge ... "Well," I said, "What do you make of that?" ... " It certainly was no hallucination, though it makes one think of the 'the Flying Dutchman'," said Mr Jansen, and I told him what had happened before he came on the scene ... "More and more puzzling" ... "Did you notice her colours, painted on her side? It was difficult to see, they were rather weatherworn. It was either blue and a yellow X, or white with a blue X, Swede or Finn. The odds are on the latter. They still have two or three large sailingships in the trade, belonging to Gustav Erikson, but her name eludes me; the *Parma* and the *Peking*, yes, but the *Preussen* ... No ..." "Why turn away?" remarked Hobbema. "Must have something to hide? ... all very queer" ... and the topic of conversation for the next few days ...

We arrived in Capetown on the 4th and had a pleasant five days there. Our agent supplied us with free picture tickets, invitations for dances and bus trips and ... free haircuts, all highly organised.

Our master was absent most of the time and slept ashore. After we had discharged our cargo, we got orders for Durban, there might be a cargo, not certain.

We passed 'The Point', at Durban into a packed bay, passed the whale factory, where a large whale was being flensed; the stench of the blubber reached us and made us feel sick, though not for long. By the time we passed the coal jetties, all was well. We spotted a Dutch flag and identified the ship as one of our company, the *Beraou*, a 5,000-ton cargoship, under the coalshoot; soon after we were berthed near West Street, the main thoroughfare. That evening, the master of the *Beraou* and his C.O. came over to us for a drink, while our captain spent the night ashore.

Of course, the *Preussen* incident was hotly discussed. Captain Cramer said he'd heard it said that Swedish ships had instructions to avoid trouble with the Germans "at all costs", strictly neutral at all times, and that could be a reason. "I think it must have been a Swede, Finland is pro-allied."

The *Beraou* left on Friday the 13th ... There was no cargo for us and we sailed two days later for Batavia.

On 21st March, we were halfway, in the centre of the Indian Ocean; the weather was perfect, windforce 3 / 4, a cool breeze from the N., a long low lazy swell, very good visibility, 10 miles or more. It was hard to believe that the world was in turmoil …

The captain and I were in the chartroom, making notes for the 'noon' position, Jansen, who is much on the bridge these lovely days, chatting with Hobbema. It was 01.05 when a long shrill whistleblast shattered the peace and we hurried to the bridge. It was from the crows' nest: the look-out, who has a pair of glasses, points to a point abeam and shouts, "I think it is a warship!" … We grab our binoculars … I vaguely find it but can't make out, something … I go to the monkey deck and look again … yes … the ship is keel down upper structure well visible … definitely, a warship … I take a bearing and go down. I call for the Serang who appears immediately, "Put on lifejackets, and all not on duty assemble at the boats and await orders." … Our Master, watching the warship, makes no comment. I tell him, "Her course is roughly due South (ours being 67). She has just asked our name by Aldis (very bright)" and the Captain says: "I'll handle this" – KALIMATI DUTCH) – only a dot as reply … we wait, the seconds ticking away – I think, "This is it, then," while putting my lifejacket on; the others have already done so. The next question certainly floors me: NAMEN KAPITAN BITTE – gasps from all around – "I am double … damned", from our Chief … "I can't believe this, too much of a coincidence," from Hobbema, and I can't find words; we all look at our master but can't see his face, he is watching with his glasses again … "Is that one of your friends again?" asks Jansen … Our captain puts his glasses down and taps: BAUER ... A long dash ... and that was all, she clearly altered course ... and some minutes later, the horizon was clear again ...

The captain turned to Jansen and me. "As to your question, the answer is 'yes', and remember this (stressing the word), "We are not at war with Germany," and with these parting words and a look on his face like a cat who had swallowed a canary, he retired to his cabin ...

Of course we were relieved, anti-climax, but Mr Bauer had to answer more questions now, and that he certainly did not do, not to us anyway. We had our own ideas though; for instance, that asking for his name had to be a code-word of some kind ... and so, his lordship had to be involved in some chicanery.

I wrote a long report, and asked all those who had been present to sign with me ... we had no proof, only suspicion, but then ...

When we arrived safely in Batavia, the marine superintendent told us that the *Beraou* had bought it not far from the coast and a humane U-boat Commander had allowed the crew to leave in the boats; they had reached the coast in due time and had contacted the Dutch consul in Durban, who had informed our H.Q.

Our story was believed and Mr Bauer was given a position in an obscure job in Pontianak, Borneo, where he could do no harm; after all we had no proof ... He was interned with hundreds of others, on the 10th May, when Germany overran the Low Countries.

8

The Miracle

By Captain Bernard Soep

This was first published as an article in the Nautical Magazine, *Vol. 227, No. 1, January 1982, and is reprinted here with the Editor's approval. See note at the end of the chapter.*

Forty years ago this January 1982, a British Army doctor, T.A., 'borrowed' a small Chinese riverboat and evacuated his whole medical unit (a casualty clearing unit) from Penang Island in Malaya. This included all his patients, 70 of whom were stretcher cases, plus some 250 civilians who, hearing of his plans, pleaded to get away before the Japanese occupied the island. So he might be considered to have been a forerunner of the present day Boat People.

The Wusueh was a typical craft, built on the lines of her much larger and more powerful sisterships on the Mississippi, except that she was propeller driven, with two rudders, in fact a self propelled houseboat, a flat bottomed contraption, built for river traffic and certainly not for the ocean. Coal burning, she provided passage for between 150 and 200 passengers and all their paraphernalia for up to three weeks, plying between Chunking and Shanghai on the Yangtse-Kiang, a distance of over 1,500 miles. Her engines were still sound, thanks to the forethought of her owner captain, the cheerful Mr Wu. He had already sailed her from Shanghai to Singapore in 1935 during the big Japanese invasion; then in 1939, when it was clear that war would reach the whole of the Far East sooner or later, he joined his brothers in Penang by sailing his 'possession' once again over there, and ... prepared himself for further developments, by keeping his engineers and ordering them to keep the engines in first class order; when he was asked, "Why?" ... he grinned ... "Me run twice ... better savie all time ..."

She had, however, not seen any drydock for over three years and her bottom was as foul as could be expected, with barnacles and long streamers of vegetation. Her speed would be nothing to shout about, perhaps seven or eight knots, but she was of sturdy construction, built to withstand the treacherous currents and whirlpools of the Yangtse-Kiang with its thousands of rocks and sandbanks. Captain Wu was supremely optimistic, knowing every plank and nail of his ship, full of confidence, perhaps more than was justified, but his cheery countenance brought hope to and inspired all hearts.

Her bridge was right forward on the bow and her smoke stack right aft, presently belching black smoke, clearly visible for at least 20 miles, all round the horizon in the clear January air of 1942. She was on her way from Penang to Colombo, 1,200 miles away: that was the intention anyway ...

Every square inch was occupied, either with stores, sacks of coal, fruit, or human beings with their spare belongings ... "just like home", grinned Captain Wu ... "and it even smells the same". They 'thought' that they had 380 passengers on board at the time of sailing, plus a crew of 16 including the patients and medical staff; nobody was sure, but the Honourable *Wusueh* had never carried more than 250 souls . . . "May the Lord keep and save us," prayed Colonel Carr, the instigator and mentor of this whole rather mad enterprise. They were the last ship to leave the almost deserted harbour, 24 hours before the arrival of the Japanese.

Destined for a very uncertain immediate future, and 10 to 14 days of a cheek by jowl existence, it was a United Nations in miniature: English, Irish and Scots, Malays, Dutch, Chinese, Australians and two American missionaries. Even on the bridge, the difference being, that here the leaders were congregated. Wu, Carr and Walker, for instance, had stretchers at the back of the huge steering wheel, while on starboard a little screen had been hung to afford some privacy for the Matron and the two Chinese Sisters. With difficulty, a little path was kept clear for the watch-keeper moving from port to starboard and vice-versa, between crates of medical supplies that the Matron very much preferred to keep her eyes on. She was quite a character, an ex linen stewardess in peacetime with P.& O., who had trained as a Nursing Sister long ago. She wore her grey hair done up with a broad blue ribbon, which nobody had ever seen her without. Short and stoutly built with ample bosom, she was always on the move, and though only proficient in Lancashire English, she was a perfect organiser and made herself understood in what she wanted done by doing it herself first. Apparently forever going without sleep, she was the perfect executor of Colonel Carr's orders and wishes.

They had no proper charts or instruments such as a sextant. The principal means of guidance, and that is all it was, was a so-called pilot chart of size 40" by 30" which gave an overall picture of the whole of the Indian Ocean from Africa to Indonesia. It showed the course and strength of prevailing currents and winds through the whole of the year, and it gave them a rough idea how to avoid running on to the Sumatran coast, and what general course to steer for Ceylon, their main goal and landfall, and to mark what progress was made, roughly that is, one inch covering 50 miles.

A highly polished binnacle contained a compass which had not been adjusted since Wu sailed from Shanghai and was therefore highly unreliable. Major Walker, ex Gurkha Rifles, who had been appointed Navigator (he had been under treatment for malaria, when the first plans were made, and had simply left his bed to offer his services), had a go at it for the first couple of hours after departure. He took numerous bearings of known landmarks in the waters around Penang and compared these with the maps in his local ordnance books and concluded that the compass was 15 to 20 degrees 'out'. For the voyage he used a 'Heath

Robinson' idea: with the aid of two small field compasses, he checked these with the ship's by observing when the sun was at its highest with a kind of Pelorus he had constructed, all roughly of course, with much guesswork and finding the approximate 'error' that had to be applied to the ship's heading. They also had a 'Walker-Cherub' log; a present from the Harbour Master, so the distance run through the water could be checked.

A course was set for Sabang, a tiny island lying off the North Point of Sumatra; if sighted straight ahead, the compass could be corrected with the calculated 'error'. This happened in due course, to Major Walker's great satisfaction, and the next landfall had to be Ceylon ... over 1,000 miles away.

Most days were overcast with plenty of short showers, followed by blazing sunshine for an hour or so. The rain was very welcome, and gave them a good supply of fresh water in the many receptacles: empty oil drums and wooden tubs, which been ordered by Walker before sailing and placed in strategic positions. The hospital staff, though small, worked efficiently, and by allocating as many volunteers as were needed for a job, whether it was cleaning decks or washing dishes, feeding patients or assisting the orderlies, it kept morale very high.

The whole enterprise and organisation was chiefly due to the man in charge, Colonel Carr, T.A. He was an eye specialist, born in Stafford, England; he had seen service with the Territorials in the First World War, from which he emerged with his present rank. Over 60 years of age, he was married; his wife and two children, who had abided by his decision "that he had to do his bit", now patiently awaited his return.

Having joined up in the autumn of 1939, he had been posted in December 1940 to the small B.M.H. in Georgetown, the capital of Penang Island. Standing at over six feet, powerfully built with wide shoulders, sparse grey hair, rather myopic, he wore thick lens spectacles perched on his ample nose, his vivid blue eyes twinkling behind his glasses. His speech was fascinating; he spoke in bursts, impatient to say what he wanted, having a most colourful and picturesque choice of words; e.g. he called all his female staff "my wenches", and always the words seemed to tumble over each other.

During rounds (his cap invariably pushed up from his forehead, his swagger stick under his arm, a shining red face), when addressing somebody he took off his glasses and polished them with an enormous, spotlessly clean white handkerchief, replaced them and moved on, slightly stooped, walking with long strides; one could picture him in tweeds and breeches as a traditional English landlord inspecting his estate.

He was kindness personified, but with a remarkably persuasive power once his mind was made up. Needless to say he had few if any enemies, and it was his presence, more than anything else, which made this mixture of people and such a divergence of natures into willing followers willing to abide by his orders and demands. Everybody trusted him and most expected a miracle from him in reaching their objective safely.

The Miracle

It was late afternoon on the sixth day after passing Sabang. Thanks to the perfect weather conditions, Major Walker estimated they were over the half way mark. All who could find a place were crowded on deck, enjoying the breeze and, as had been urged, talking in a low muted voice, mostly concerning the future, once safely in India. Many watched the breathtaking display provided by nature, continuous distant lightning at the horizon, too far to be heard; short heavy showers could be seen, only occasionally hitting the ship. Vividly bright phosphorescence added to this fairytale-like performance. The showers seemed like the broad shafts of dark fingers groping from the sky towards the earth, and where they reached the ocean surface brilliant white patches showed as if pinpointed by floodlight. This heavenly play kept all enthralled by its sheer beauty. Added to this, the long lazy swell, all the way from Africa, caused the ship to roll and pitch continuously, giving an almost sensual feeling, and most felt nearly contented, while they puff-puffed along at the leisurely pace of seven knots, leaving its signature of dots and dashes far astern.

The bridge was very alert and a strict lookout was kept at all times, especially so at sunrise and sunset. No lack of volunteers, but a certain skill was essential – good eyesight, the ability to concentrate and stay awake for two hours at a time, each spell of duty, eight people in all, 24 hours of the day, positioned four on either side, in addition to the Captain and officer on watch. Both Colonel Carr and Major Walker every dawn and sunset did their own lookout, using their binoculars and always together.

On this particular occasion they stood a short distance from the bridge on starboard side; the Colonel leaned with his back against the railing, cursing under his breath, wiping his binoculars vigorously with his large handkerchief, while the Major, facing him, was scanning the horizon from dead astern to starboard abeam. He lowered his glasses a moment, holding them against his life jacket, while he watched the frolics of a school of dolphins overtaking them, dozens of slick streamlined bodies ... out of the water ... in again, hardly with a ripple of the surface; one never tired watching this play ... happy cigar-shaped creatures ... they resembled ... while in the water ... torpedoes.

He lifted his binoculars again to resume his look out ... almost immediately: "Good God," he whispered hoarsely ... "those are not dolphins, they are bloody torpedoes."

Notwithstanding the whisper, Carr heard him, turned like a flash, brought his binoculars to bear and swore when he confirmed what Walker saw ... two tracks, one slightly behind the other ... fast overtaking them – the phosphorescent trails marked them accurately; no jumps out of the water here ... so near already that no alarm could give any reasonable amount of warning ... still ... he turned towards the bridge, brought his hands to his mouth, when at that precise moment, he saw the ship swinging to port: the bridge had spotted the missiles aimed at the ship with deadly accuracy; he saw Wu and two other men peering through their own glasses towards the stern. Two death- and destruction-bringing objects, racing at 30 to 35 m.p.h. against the ship's puny seven knots, 500 lb of T.N.T. each, and anything that might be done within the next five to seven seconds (Walker's guess) would be utterly useless ... except for Wu's alertness ... the stern swung agonisingly slowly towards the course of the torpedo tracks, narrowing the gap. Wu's immediate reaction had been to order hard aport, the old lady had responded to the rudders ... she did her level best ... but her speed was slow ... her bottom foul ... it was the only possible manoeuvre to present the least possible width of target ... a desperate effort ... chance of success one in a million.

'No chance whatsoever,' went through the two soldiers' minds, who judged with their trained eyes the narrowing angle with the speed of the torpedoes.

"This is it, David," said Walker. "I am afraid so," answered Carr, adding "Ian" as an afterthought, both using each other's Christian name for the first and probably the last time in their relationship.

Almost immediately shouts and yells came from the port side ... the two men gazed at each other in utter disbelief ... more shouting from the bridge, they saw Wu, swinging his arms and hopping madly up and down, but the resulting din of noise was now so loud that they could not make out what he said, they were only aware of the fact that the *Wusueh* was still moving along, completely unconcerned by what had happened, as she had done for the last six days.

At first they thought that the torpedoes had missed. "Impossible, we both saw them find their mark, behind amidships," shouted Carr ... then realisation of the truth, the wonderful truth, dawned on them: "They passed UNDER the ship," and they grasped each other's shoulders ... "They were set to hit an ordinary ship," and Walker laughed his head off, joined by the Colonel, who in the general confusion of joy had his hat and glasses knocked off and could only recover by blowing his nose in his big white handkerchief.

The destructors had passed under the *Wusueh*, set for a depth of 12 to 15 feet for a normal small target, but the old riverboat had a depth of 10 feet only, and .... very important ... had a flat bottom.

The two men made their way to the bridge, struggling through the excited passengers, who did not really understand what had happened, something miraculous :.. an escape ... and found that Wu had already reverted to the previous course ... "We stand a fair chance of not being seen any more, the Jap will not expect us to do just that," he grinned. "Look see ... rain come all over the place," and as if by Royal Command, a sudden heavy squall hit them.

Whatever the case, no more attacks took place that night. The *Wusueh* continued her unhurried voyage, though all were full of anxiety and apprehension during the remaining hours of darkness. Perhaps the enemy thought his intended victim not too important, and he had lost two precious torpedoes already.

Nobody slept that night. The people that had seen the torpedoes emerge from under the ship at portside and

Teamwork, 1920s

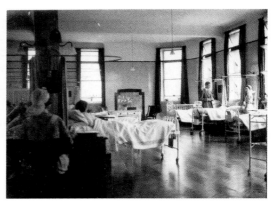

Marion on duty at
St Barts, 1930s

Medical Ward at St Barts, 1930s

Graduation from St Barts 1936/37.
Front row, left to right: unknown, Butler, Mazie Calcutt, unknown,
Matron Helen Dey, M. Beazley, Marian Roger, unknown,
Kathleen Raven.
Middle row, left to right: Joan Loveridge, Kay Roberts, unknown,
unknown, M.D. Godson, E.J. Heitland.
Top row, left to right: J.L. Percy, and others not identified
with certainty.

Sister Marion Roger, Q.A.I.M.N.S. (R.)

Two Q.A.I.M.N.S. Sisters (Marion a Reserve) flanking a Red Cross Sister, Cambridge Hospital, Aldershot, 1941 (illustrating variance in uniform)

Members of the 9th C.C.S. en route to Bombay, aboard S.S. *Johan van Oldenbarnavelt*, March 1942

Marion en route to Bombay, March 1942

Ninth C.C.S. at Ahmadnagar, near Bombay. Matron Meade is on the right.

By buggy around Ahmadnagar, 1942

Locals at Ahmadnagar

Kanchenjunga from Sandakphu at sunrise

Marion on horseback at
Darjeeling

Train from Siliguri to
Darjeeling: the engine was
Glasgow-built

Kippi, Marion's personal
Sherpa

Marion, Kippi and the boys,
1942

The rosary given to
Marion

Marion's tent at Sandakphu

Source of the rosary

"I promise, Sister, I'll go back to bed!" Marion at Ranchi, 2 October 1942

Medical staff tents at Nan Comb, Ranchi

Ninth C.C.S. at Ranchi, near Calcutta. Miss Wilkinson (Principal Matron for India), centre.

S.S. *Melchior Treub*, lounge

Recreation on board S.S. *Melchior Treub*

S.S. *Melchior Treub*

Hospital Ship No. 6 at Chittagong, 1944

Hospital Ship No. 6: ship's officers, surgical and medical staff.
Front row (L to R) Surgeon? Matron Meade, Col. Carr, Captain?
Chief Engineer? Sister Roger, M.O. Stanley.
Middle row: Unknown orderlies, nurses, ship's officers and
M.O.s. Chief Officer Bernard Soep, centre (behind Captain).
Back row: unknown medical orderlies.

Hospital Ship No. 6 staff

Hospital Ship No. 6: Ship's medical staff

S.S. *Wusueh*, subject of 'The Miracle'

S.S. *Wusueh* team, 1942. Left to right:
Surgeon (Major), Chief Officer,
Captain Wu (owner), Sister Syme,
Colonel Carr.

Casualty embarkation by dukw at Maundaw, 1945

Marion, second from left, with others on horseback, January 1943

Ramree Isle Hospital (ex-jail): Marion in centre

Stuck horse on the return from
Sebu La

Ranikhet,
September 1944

Leaving Jessie at Thangu, July 1944.
Back row: Marion, extreme left; Stanley, third
from left; Bernard, fourth from right; Jessie,
extreme right.

Victory Parade in Singapore, V.J. Day, August 1945

Bernard Soep at
the time of his
Engagement on
return from the
'2nd Trek',
Calcutta, July
1945

The Soep family
with a friend in
Maracaibo,
Venezuela

Marion W.
Roger at the
time of her
Engagement,
Calcutta, 1945.
At the end of
her 2nd Trek,
Marion
weighed six
stones.

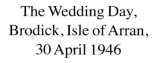

A possible item, 1945

The Wedding Day,
Brodick, Isle of Arran,
30 April 1946

Guide Patrol. Top left: Dunagoil Bay, Bute. Top right: Retiral from Guiding. Bottom left and right: Hafton, Hunters Quay.

The staff of Rankin Maternity Hospital celebrate Christmas.
Photograph reprinted by courtesy of Norman Burniston and
Greenock Telegraph.

Right: Marion as Acting Matron of Glenfield Medical Aid Home. Her contribution to Glenfield during her two years in this post was acknowledged in the glowing tributes she received from colleagues and patients on her retiral. Photograph reprinted by courtesy of Norman Burniston and *Greenock Telegraph*.

...ves surprise Matron Marion

and then old folk in an Soep nursed them both

...aff gathered to do her hon-...ur. Her husband had also ...een invited secretly and she ...as completely over-...helmed.

The watch was presented ...y Sister Sandra Blair, who ...as now taken over as ...atron, with Margaret ...amieson as her depute.

It is interesting to know ...hat Mrs Soep did with her ...wo gift cheques.

She said: "I rushed out ...nd bought a music centre. ...t was lovely having money ...o spend on such a luxury. I ...new it was now or never. If ...I had waited I would have ...ought of a more practical ...se for the money."

Before coming to Glen-...eld, Mrs Soep was at Ran-...in Hospital for 14 years as ...ard sister, night sister, and ...or the last three years as ...linical tutor.

An excellent summing-up ...f her character was given ...hen she retired from Ran-...in Hospital in October 1978 ...y Mr James Baker, Director ...f Nurse Education, In-...erclyde and Bute College of ...ursing and Midwifery.

INTERESTS

He said: "Her hard-...orking professionalism and ...er-flowing enthusiasm for ...ursing has always been ...omething quite splendid."

Mrs Soep and husband

Bernard live at 11 Golf Road, Gourock. They have two married sons, John and Rog-er, and two grandchildren.

She is a woman of wide interests, and is an ex-Girl Guide Division Commis-sioner, and is a member of the Toastmistress Club and League of Hospital Friends.

ONCE a nurse, always a nurse, and Mrs Marion Soep has lived in uniform for the best part of her life.

Ninety years young:
Bernard (top) and Marion celebrate their
ninetieth birthdays.
Pictured with Marion at the Ardgowan
Hospice are son John and his wife Carol.

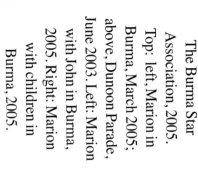

The Burma Star
Association, 2005.
Top: left, Marion in
Burma, March 2005;
above, Dunoon Parade,
June 2003. Left: Marion
with John in Burma,
2005. Right: Marion
with children in
Burma, 2005.

continue their journey into nowhere had to tell their story over and over again – how they could not believe their eyes – this was the absolute miracle all had been praying for that Colonel Carr would produce. Nothing would change that opinion ... this would be told for generations to come ... if, of course, and this was still a big If, they arrived safely ... and as G. B. Shaw has written, "A miracle is an event when faith is born."

When dawn broke under a clear blue sky, with hardly a ripple on the ocean surface, but only the long swell, every soul was too tired to stay awake and a Sunday-like atmosphere hung over the entire ship. Only the hospital staff and crew attended to their never ending duties; the lookouts remained sharp, even more alert after last night's event ... but the fright had been real, and nobody removed their life jacket to sleep on.

Three days later, Adam's Peak was sighted, 7,370 feet high, the top showing at sunset above the clouds, 20 degrees on the starboard bow.

Major Walker was very happy, calculating his error as approximately 30 miles off the true position ... not bad at all, he asserted smugly. (He realised afterwards that he never had taken the current under scrutiny.) "Still 130 miles to go," he said. "Tomorrow afternoon." It was glorious night, full moon, few slept; now certainly all danger was past. Though they were already within an hour's flying from the island, he had no radio to ask for assistance if needed.

But all went well, and so one began to realise, slowly at first, that the gamble had come off. Captain Wu could not refrain from saying, "I told you so," with his likeable grin from ear to ear, showing his many gold teeth ("my investment").

When at last they tied up in Colombo harbour, all hospital cases were quickly landed, but it was another fortnight before every passenger had been vetted and sorted out ... many had no passport, only a scrap of 'official' paper of sorts.

The crew remained intact, as was the medical staff, thanks to the Colonel, who showed his usual tenacity and verbosity to keep his wenches together.

When orders came to sail for Bombay, no passengers were allowed – the high ups did not consider it safe enough. The *Wusueh* arrived in Bombay on the 15th February, the day Singapore surrendered.

Note

During research into documentation in the course of writing this book, it was realised that the original author, Captain Bernard Soep, omitted to use certain correct names. Colonel Carr was referred to as Colonel Stewart and the Wusueh was referred to as the Cho Sun.

9

Hospital Ship No. 6

By Captain Bernard Soep

This was first published as an article in the Nautical Magazine, *Vol. 236, No. 5, November 1986, and is reprinted here with the Editor's approval.*

She was small for a passenger ship, some 4,000 tons, but she had graceful lines. In peacetime she had seen service as one of the 'kapal poetih' (white ships) maintaining a regular weekly service between Belawan Deli in N. Sumatra, Singapore and Java.

She had a good speed for her time, over 14 knots p/h, and was very nicely fitted out with a large beautiful saloon and dining room, which could sit over 100 passengers and had accommodation for 60 first class, 24 second class and about 200 deck passengers.

When Singapore fell, the loss of Indonesia was just a matter of time and the decision was taken to disperse our fleet of some 150 ships as soon as possible, without entirely isolating the almost 200 islands of the

Archipelago who depended on free communication as their lifeline.

Australia and India were the obvious choice, and because Holland had been occupied and our government was now seated in London, all ships came under orders from the Ministry of War and Transport (M.W.T.) in London, retaining their Dutch nationality and flying the Dutch flag.

The *Melchior Treub* was ordered to Bombay and anchored in the Bay behind Elephant Island in March '42. But it was October before the *Treub* received her first orders for trooping and I was posted to her. For the next six months we trooped between Karachi in the North and Colombo in the south, with Bombay as base, and in April next we became officially attached to the Indian army fighting in Burma and ferried between Calcutta and Chittagong. Delhi had the bright idea to use us for fully armed troops on the way out and taking casualties back. This was of course all wrong, and we would be liable to enemy-attack when having wounded on board only. All were walking cases, mostly suffering from malaria, mixed with men going on leave, and that is how we came to know Colonel Carr. We had become more or less a transport detachment of the 14th army, which was fighting its come-back in Burma, and Colonel Carr had been in charge and insisted that they were not covered by the Geneva Convention when carrying patients. That was why it was decided to convert a troopship to a hospital ship.

We came to know him as a very remarkable personality. As soon as he became aware how the ship was used, he almost blew a blood vessel and asked to see the Captain: "This is outrageous and I will see that something is done about it," and he did . . . He went to Delhi and brought his case before the C-in-C and carried the day. He told us afterwards, that he won mainly because he convinced the 'powers that be' that the Dutch officers give their 100% co-operation Anyway, the result was that the *Treub* was going to be converted into a hospital ship as soon as possible, and so it was . . . in September we got our orders and entered Calcutta for the conversion. The work would be carried out by the Garden Reach Workshop, a Scots surveyor in charge with a government official for the medical aspect. Later, Colonel Carr arrived to protect his side and advise on staff matters etc. This did not go well with the Surveyor: "The bl.... man is just a blooming nuisance, he wants a modern hospital ship, and my orders are for a hospital carrier, more or less a floating ambulance for short trips of no more than three days' duration: no X-ray. No big theatre, just enough facilities to keep the wounded comfortable ... " and Colonel Carr fumed at the mouth, but at the end of each day they enjoyed a drink together.

He was already in his sixties, a big man, over six feet, wide-shouldered and an eye specialist in civil life. He had had a practice in Singapore when war broke out and had immediately joined up. Once we knew him better, we slowly drew his story of his escape out of him (see my story "The Miracle" in the *Magazine* of Jan. '82): how he had talked the owner of a Chinese riverboat into taking him and his entire unit of nearly a

100 (inc. casualties) to the safety of Colombo. He wore glasses and when discussing a point would invariably take these off and polish them with a huge spotless white handkerchief while talking with spasms of speech and squinting at his listener. When we lost our name and became officially No. 6, he became our official M.O. in charge.

We had the good fortune to have him on board for well over two years. One of his habits was to call his female staff "my wenches", and if any newcomer took any offence at this, it was pointed out that this really was an expression of endearment. He was adored by his staff and did not have any enemies as far as we knew.

In two months' hard work in Matia Bruz (dockyard in Calcutta), most of our first class was stripped or broken out and converted into two wards. Some second class cabins were maintained for the eight medical orderlies, all British. When completed, Hospital Ship No. 6 had one medical ward, one surgical and an isolation ward (on the poop), one office and one room with an operation table for small surgery. The staff could all be accommodated in the remaining first class cabins around the large saloon. By the time the ship was ready, we had: one Lt. Col. (Br), one Major Medical BR one Capt. Surgeon (Br), three Indian Drs, one Br. Matron, three Br. Sisters and two Indian nurses plus eight B.O.R.s [British Other Ranks] and, to round off, 60 I.O.R.s [Indian Other Ranks] in addition to two British wireless-operators familiar with military signalling. We could cope with 300 wounded at the time and more if needed; during the height of the battle of Kohima on several trips, 340. For the convenience of ward 1 (the walking cases) eight 'loos' had been built in the forward well deck. They were rather flimsy, made from steel with corrugated iron roofs, most uncomfortable for the users: spray coming over the bow, rained down on the men... and once... when we struck bad weather, the whole set-up was smashed; more about that later. By a great coincidence, we discovered that our Matron was from England, one Sister from Scotland, one from Wales and one from Ireland, and what with the Indian staff and Javanese crew, Dutch Officers, Guyanese catering personnel, a truly United Nations; four languages had to be spoken at all times to make this into ONE Unit; Urdu, English, Dutch and Malay.

The entire ship had been painted white, replacing the dull wartime grey. For night time, we had been fitted with a string of lights contained in a wooden casing, protected by glass, around the superstructure above the line of windows, with the exception of the bridgehouse, plus four floodlights at the base of the funnel with the large red crosses. At night we would sail with everything switched on, all according to the Geneva Convention, signed by most countries in 1864.

We had to cope with different sects and customs, because of religion: Muslim, Hindu, Buddhists, Christians and Brahmans, Untouchables and Parsees, poles apart. Our Indian staff explained what was customary and we all tried to be as conciliatory as possible.

After a couple of months, a common sense of purpose began to emerge and all was welded into one working community. For instance, the Brahmans and the Untouchables amongst the I.O.R.s worked side by side cleaning ship, sweeping the decks, working on holy days, sharing food. Though having their own cook, it was prepared in the same galley, using the same pots and pans. To go ahead a bit: in the spring of '44, we had the great honour to be inspected by Field-Marshal Sir Claude Auchinleck, at very short notice, a couple of hours before departure, and all preparatory work had to continue. When the Field-Marshal went through the wards, he saw our Javanese crew (Muslim) side by side with I.O.R.s (Buddhists), holystoning the deck and expressed his astonishment how this was achieved ... our medical staff were very proud people that day.

By the middle of December, Hospital Ship No. 6 was ready for her task and was officially taken over. The *Times of India* proclaimed with a whole page advert: "The latest and most modern Hospital Ship for the Indian Army will be open to the public on the 20th Dec. '43 ..."

When in port, it was daily practice of our Captain to do the rounds with the Second Engineer, myself and the boatswain at 10.00 a.m. On one of these walks we passed the theatre and medical office and saw the Sister (the Scottish) on all fours vigorously scrubbing the concrete floor. The captain called out whether it was really necessary to do this herself as he found it rather undignified ... "Oh, good morning, Captain. No to your question, all are otherwise engaged." "Well," said the Master, "in future be so kind as to let the Chief Officer know when you are short of manpower and he will surely help you out for anything at all." And I can say, she certainly did; she has been my wife now for over 40 years...

As a girl, she had 'messed about with boats' and earned her badge as boatswain in the Guides. Everything had to be made 'storm proof': she borrowed our carpenter, and a framework of fiddles was made for the tables, the sterilised surgical instruments and all the glassware such as syringes. The end-product was a masterpiece of improvisation; breakages were rare. Last but not least, the operation table was anchored into the concrete floor.

We received our sailing-orders on Christmas Eve and left next morning for Chittagong, total distance from Calcutta and return 765 miles, our average voyage covered four to five days.

It was remarkably well timed: we noticed, when in Chittagong, a large build-up of troops and supplies, and rumours were aplenty of the coming 'Big Push' to drive the Japanese back from where they came. It had indeed already started, though we did not know it then; in the middle of December the operation was in full swing from Ledo in the far North, in the back of the enemy in order to disrupt their lines of communication with the Arakan, and here the big attack started on the 19th January, southwards, along the coast. At first all went well, thick mud and malaria being the worst enemies; advances of up to five miles a day were made, but the

15th Corps under General Christison was of good cheer: the Japanese were at last driven back.

The enemy was not caught napping. With ten divisions at their disposal along a line from East of Kohima in the North to Arakan in the South, they counter-attacked on the 4th February, and within days our southern flank was all but surrounded. Mountbatten was up to the challenge: he begged and borrowed a large fleet of American transport planes, and all supplies were delivered to them by air. The Japanese did not have this back up. Their high command had equipped them with two weeks' supply of everything, confident of victory within that time, and counted on the ample stores they would find in Chittagong. Christison broke them up into small groups, forcing them to retreat; by the 1st March the ring was broken and we achieved our first victory in Burma. The count of dead the enemy left behind was over 5,000. They carried their wounded away with them, the story being that those that fell into the allies' hands were shot. Meantime we kept pace with the battle and made some trips during February with over-capacity of some 320 stretcher cases. We even used the forward ward for them, the walking cases giving their beds. Most of our badly wounded were flown out, the not so serious ones were shipped by train and the remainder by sea, but we still carried over 1,000 surgical cases during a period of four weeks.

It was during this period that the first Japanese prisoners were taken, and also some wounded were left behind. P.O.W.s or not, all received the same treatment, white or yellow, black or brown. It was not all grim. We had lighter moments, such as the time when a Gurkha needing a transfusion was propped up in bed and saw a Japanese opposite him at the other side of the ward. He shouted "Japoni, where is my kukri, I'll kill him." He struggled to get out of bed but could not free himself from his attached drip. Sister told him to behave himself, and the Gurkha on guard at the prisoners' side came over to order him down in his own language. The Japanese was unruffled; he just grinned at the sight of his worst enemy. And then we had the case of the 'Hara-kiri'. Again a Japanese provided the amusement. The M.O. in the C.C.S. wrote his report: 'When found, the wounded, an officer, committed 'hara-kiri' by thrusting his sword into his chest into the place he expected his heart to be, but by a fluke it was not there. When hit near the heart a bullet had caused extensive bleeding but blood could not get away and stayed in a kind of sac, pushing the heart aside ... By stabbing himself there, he pierced the sac, the blood escaped and actually relieved the pressure while he lost consciousness to wake up in our C.C.S., and a very surprised man he was. Through an interpreter the matter was explained to him, he struggled to his feet, bowed solemnly three times and said: "Me vely happy man" – all the English he could muster. His honour had been saved, he told the interpreter.

After the success in the Arakan, the larger battle was to come; on the 8th March, the enemy attacked our entire central front with three divisions toward Imphal and Kohima and the railway from Dinapur in the N.F.

corner of India, our main supply route. During the next three weeks our troops were gradually pushed back and Kohima was slowly surrounded, the situation became daily more critical, the garrison had been reduced to three battalions plus everyone who could bear arms, even the convalescent from the hospital.

On the 4th April all was reduced to a single hill . . . Mountbatten again pleaded for massive air-support and got it. All activities in the Arakan were stopped and the entire 5th Indian Division was airlifted by the Americans, urgent supplies were dropped by parachute, even donkeys, ammunition and field guns, reinforcements arrived by train and fought their way from the west, 60 miles to Kohima and the beleaguered and dead tired troops were relieved on the 20th April; the Japanese were driven back far beyond.

This took all of eight weeks till on the 22nd June Lord Mountbatten reported to Churchill, "The Japanese bid for India is virtually over . . ."

Of course, we had been very busy, especially in March and the first half of April; we even managed two trips during the last week of March carrying a total of over 1,000 wounded within 10 days. This was exceptionally good as the weather had gradually deteriorated, the Monsoon was arriving. This influx seemed to be more than the hospital services in Calcutta could cope with and on the 10th April we were redirected from Chittagong to Madras, some 1,000 miles to the south, taking over 72 hours, a challenge for our overworked medical staff. Strangely enough though, they preferred these long voyages; they could take better care of their charges. And it was one of these trips – No. 6 was very lively, rain was pelting down – that I received a little message from our surgeon: "Please, could you possibly keep the ship steady for 15 minutes or so? I have an amputation to perform and it is rather awkward under these conditions." I told the Captain, we reduced speed, altered course and 'hove to'. It had the required effect; 15 minutes later we could resume our voyage. Next day there came a request for a blood donor; the amputee had lost too much; and I volunteered. Seemingly with great success: Captain Chapman, our surgeon, told us that when the Scottish soldier was carried off in Madras, one of the bearers stumbled and the Scot swore in fluent Dutch . . .

Embarkation in Chittagong depended entirely on the tide; we could only be alongside during high water for two to three hours because of the shallowness of the riverbed, so everything had to be highly organised.

Available: one narrow gangway heavy enough and safe for the purpose of carrying stretchers with occupants along. Each case had a large coloured label pinned on his chest with a short description of his case, for instance: red for surgical, blue for medical and yellow for isolation. When passing the sergeant at the gangway, he called out where to go after checking the label. This worked fine and smoothly in good weather, but if it was blowing with pelting rain, it could be difficult. We moored alongside the shed where the wounded had been carried in; at least the men were dry there, sometimes having to wait several hours before we had arrived, but even then when we started the embarkation in pouring rain, the men were remarkably cheerful and cracking jokes about the soaking they got, apart from the shake up caused by the pace the loading had to be done at. One day this coincided with lunchtime, so everybody gave a hand. Even Colonel Carr helped carrying food over to the wards. As he was crossing the open deck from the cookhouse, with a full plate in each hand filled with sausages, tomatoes and mashed potatoes, three or four large gulls swooped down on him from a large group hovering overhead, quickly emptied the plates and covered our friend with mashed food in doing so.

The result was pandemonium – he threw plastic plates on deck, grabbed his cap with one hand and his spectacles with the other and let go a stream of profanity for at least a full minute, never repeating himself, shaking his hands at the birds, who seemingly understood him, screeched and circled and dived en masse above his head having a whale of a time fighting with the perpetrators of this foul deed to relieve them of their loot . . . All human traffic stopped and those understanding English, and even those who did not, watched and listened in open admiration; nobody had ever heard anything like it, what a performance . . .

Just as suddenly as he started, he stopped, seeing the stoppage of traffic he was causing, and shifted his anguish, and all movement resumed; the birds disappeared as if by magic. This event boosted morale immeasurably; the loading of over 300 stretcher cases was completed within one-and-a-half hours, and all had their meal on time.

The decision to build 'loos' in the forward well deck, four on each side, was taken reluctantly, an absolute necessity for the over 100 walking cases from No. 1 between deck. It was recognised as most uncomfortable for the calls of nature with the risk of spray coming over or worse, but was reasoned as being the only place, and after all, the men were used to much worse in the jungle.

One day in May, bound for Madras with a full load on board, we ran into heavy weather and during the night had to reduce speed on account of the heavy pitching, taking several nose dives, shipping tons of water and, though wind force was only 6 to 7, the seas increased and by mid-morning we took real big ones which slammed down on the structure and gradually destroyed the lot. Fortunately, nobody was caught or injured, though a number were surprised literally 'with their pants down', but escaped with a soaking.

The tangle was such that further use was impossible and dangerous, and the Captain's decision to turn for Calcutta was later commended by the Lloyds' surveyor as "very wise ... drastic structural changes were needed to avoid further mishaps." He recommended dry dock to have a 'look-see' underneath and the nearest estimate of time involved was four to five weeks. The Captain suggested that this was a golden opportunity to catch up with some leave, and Colonel Carr agreed wholeheartedly. It was Sister Roger (the Scot) who suggested a trek in the Himalayas; she had done this a couple of years before all on her own, organised by a gentleman in Darjeeling, the editor of the *Darjeeling Times*.

And so it came about that on the 1st June, a party consisting of Captain Chapman, the Matron, Sister Roger and myself, entrained in Calcutta for Siliguri at the start of a most glorious and energetic expedition that took us to a height of 17,800 feet, the Sebu La, the gateway into Tibet . . . but that of course is quite a different story . . .

10

Trek from Darjeeling to Sebu La (17,600 ft)

Extracts from Marion Soep's Diary

4–25 July 1944

DARJEELING – 7,000 ft

Tuesday 4 July 1944

We arrived in Darjeeling today by car from Siliguri, where we left the big train. It was a fine drive up, but there was little view. It was simply glorious to leave the heat behind and feel chilly at last, with mists wrapping us round. Half way up we stopped for breakfast at Kurseong, it was grand to see the cheery hill folk again, bustling round with broad grins on their faces.

We were in Darjeeling at 10.30 a.m. and while Chapman and Matron (hereafter known as Stanley and Jessie) watched the luggage, Bernard and I made for Mr Kydd to see what accommodation had been arranged. Mr Kydd arranged both my other treks. He is quite a character, an ex-schoolmaster with a fiery temper but also a heart of gold, and once he takes an interest in anyone there is no limit to what he will do.

He was busy poring over the letter I had written to him with a perfect jumble of requests and ifs etc. We had decided on one route and then on further advice changed to another, so the poor man was busy trying to sort it all out and cancel and rebook bungalows. He looked up as we entered and at once recognised me. I introduced Bernard and then he greeted me with, "Well, here you are, the greatest plague in India!"

Finally we were all assembled, plus luggage, and a great conference took place. After an hour we emerged all fixed up; at least we had planned what we wanted to do. There were all sorts of complications about passes. Sikkim is a separate state and the Maharaja takes a poor view of too many folks wandering round and particularly dying quietly on his mountains, hence vast comprehensive medical certificates are required. We had to state, amongst other items, our waist line! A battery of telegrams was sent off to the Political Officer at Gantok; he is the British representative. We hope he will provide the necessary passes when we arrive there.

We met our Sirdar today and he seemed a good sort. He is the head man and also organises the cooking etc. This one, Gylgen by name, has been on Everest and Kanchenjunga. The others look a good crowd and full of beans at the prospect of a long trek.

We are away for 19 days and have hopes of reaching 17,600 feet over the Sebu La in North Sikkim. It is a bit ambitious so we only hope it works out.

Bed calls though it is only 9 pm; how incredible it is to think it is only 24 hours since we left Calcutta.

108

Jessie and I are staying at the New Women's Services Club. It is run by the Y.W.C.A and is most comfortable. It used to be a place for novices of the sisterhood but was given up for the duration. There are fine big living rooms and verandas downstairs. The two girls running it have made it most attractive with gay cushions, curtains and chair covers. In the old days the novices had one wooden chair each and it was carried from the dining room to the sitting room. They were allowed a piano. Upstairs there is a long veranda and the rooms open on to it with another door to an inside corridor. Every couple of rooms has a middle wall not quite up to the top, making it two cubicles.

However, it is very comfortable, and each room is done in a different colour scheme. We have all this for R 7/- (10/-) per day, which is pretty good for nowadays.

DARJEELING – 7,000 ft
Wednesday 5 July 1944
I have had a great day, we spent the first part of the morning doing further arranging etc., and then I went off to see Josie. I had lunch in the mess with her and then we walked and talked our heads off. It was good to see her again, but she was not looking too well for living and working out here. But I am afraid it is the duration for all of us unless we are very sick indeed or cashiered!

Bernard came down and fetched me back, first having tea in the mess. Josie was so pleased to meet a Dutchman again after our trip out on the *J.V.O.*

Bernard and Stanley came to dinner with us. They have just gone off and we have done the odd spot of organising for the packing in the morning. Funnily enough two girls I knew at Aldershot are here. One, Duffy, with an adorable babe of four months, and the other, Thomson, about to have twins.

This morning we were called at 8.00 a.m. with breakfast in bed – what luxury! – such attractive trays with those little woollen tea cosies we used to knit at school.

BADAMTAN – 2,500 ft
Thursday 6 July 1944 (7 miles)
At last the final efforts and the porters all seen off at 10.00 a.m., after much repacking on Mr Kydd's front doorstep, each of us trying to decide what could be left out. Mr Kydd is an amusing soul, but rather tends to persuade folk that they don't need anything at all with them. "What, four blankets, nonsense! When on Everest they only used two!" At long and at last they were all off, except our Sirdar, and he came up with us to wait while we had a light lunch. We certainly looked quite a party in shorts and hefty boots. Many rather horrified and pitying looks were cast at us in the restaurant.

We left finally at 1.00 p.m. in a perfect deluge or rain. Our Sirdar was seen off by his wife and small girl, and then to Badamtan.

Our path lay steadily downhill for seven miles and a drop of 4,500 ft, a pretty easy afternoon but ah, so wet and slippery. I was most thankful for my nails. After our last trek I had a very heavy pair of nailed shoes and a pair of boots made, and I was glad I had them ready. We descended through several tea estates, mostly with Scots names, one being Bannockburn.

The bungalow we reached at 4.00 p.m., all soaked to the skin. We were soon enjoying hot tea and, after a wash and change, our first big meal. Gylgen did very well with the cooking.

We fed on dahl soup and bully beef (cold) and vegetables followed by cocoa. We left the sitting room festooned with clothes to dry. It was a lovely evening and we sat out and watched the view, the moon rising, but all too soon the mist shrouded everything.

By 9.00 p.m. all members of the expedition were snoring.

NAMCHI – 5,200 ft
Friday 7 July 1944 (11 miles)

A really eventful day. During breakfast the Sirdar told us that one man was sick with a stomach ache, so we viewed him and he did seem pretty wretched, poor fellow. He was very fed up at the idea of being left behind, as he was a real enthusiast and had done quite a bit of climbing. It was obvious, however, that he was not fit to carry a load. There was a telephone at a tea estate 1,000 feet up, so Bernard and I set off with the Chaukidar, that is the man who keeps the bungalow, and phoned Mr Kydd. He arranged to have two more porters come and pick up the load, leaving us someone to carry the oddments.

It was a very hot climb up but we soon ran down again and the entire party set off at 10.00 a.m. It was a lovely morning, clear and giving us some fine views of the valleys.

We descended through woods 1,000 feet to the R. Rangit. This is the boundary between Bengal and Sikkim. The policeman took our passes and then over the bridge. It is a suspension one and over quite a large river, flowing very swiftly – a good one for fishing I believe.

Our way then led up and up and up, some 4,000 ft over eight miles, but my word, it was some pull. I think it is about our worst day, being so out of training and so warm too. It was steep in many places. Poor Jessie was in great distress with her knees, but insisted on keeping going. However, later on it was too bad, so Stanley stopped behind with Jessie, and Bernard and I hurried on to catch up Gylgen and he arranged for a pony to go back. The two of us reached the bungalow at 4.00 pm and had time to organise hot water and tea before the others arrived, Jessie on her steed! It was a pack pony, and she had replaced two sacks of potatoes, remaining sitting on one. By this time it was a case of whether her knees or tail were in the worse state.

This is a lovely bungalow, very big; a large veranda joins the two wings, each with two double rooms and sitting room. We tried to get a pony for Jessie as far as Gantok and an old man appeared with a lovely grey animal, fat as butter and very full of life. I tried him out round the garden and he fairly went. He certainly should not get too tired. He rejoices in the name of 'Chitty'.

We had a great sing-song on the veranda; Jessie had brought a book of 'Soldiers Songs' and it contained all the favourites.

Once more the fireplace is festooned with clothes to dry. Tonight we had pumpkin soup and salmon pie. Poor Jessie and Bernard had a long wait for bedding rolls and we had begun to despair of ever seeing them. The porters had left Darjeeling early this morning and should have made it all right, as the first seven miles to Badamtan without a load is all downhill. Stanley and I between us fixed Jessie and Bernard up with odd garments. There was a great rejoicing when the porters appeared at last at 7.00 p.m. Dear me, what a forlorn pair they look. Certainly they don't seem worthy of the title of porter. They just look a very poor type of coolie. One seems to be lame and having one leg shorter than the other. I hope they can keep up with us.

TEMI – 5,000 ft
Saturday 8 July 1944 (11 miles)

Today was a pretty easy march. Down a little and then a steady climb up a good path. There were some lovely views of the valleys between the rain. Jessie was ahead on her steed and we found her at Damthang ensconced in the shelter of a house and several interested villagers looking on. We were offered a little stool each and we did appreciate getting out of the rain to have our lunch. It is easier today as with the extra porter we can have one to carry the food and oddments, extra clothes etc. Ila, being the next senior, has been given the job. He is older than the others and has had quite a lot of experience though he looks a bit past it now. He is of a Lama family and wears the special hat, a rounded affair of mauve silk brocade, crowned with a cross in red beads. He seems to have a bit of foot trouble and is always taking off either shoes or boots and going bare footed for a while.

We had our introduction to leeches today and they were quite bad enough, especially when taking to the mountains! Everywhere in the long wet grass und undergrowth they are to be found. They are similar to those used in the hospital. These are black and vary in size from small thread-like beings to about an inch long. They have a mouth each end and with these they move along. They have a very acute sense of smell and even if you sit in the middle of a rock on a wet day or after rain, they will appear from all quarters and make for you, climbing up your boots and then down the eyelets or over the tops. Wool or puttees do not deter them, they go right through, but anything as fine as silk stockings holds them up. Later we discovered the best thing was to have a stick with a bag of salt tied on the end: just a touch of that and the leech dropped off. If you pull them off they leave a mark and it bleeds furiously for as much as half an hour. The leech injects some substance into the blood to stop it clotting and it takes a time to counteract the effect. In the evening when we got in, the first job was to de-leech on the veranda (as it caused such a mess). Sometimes we made quite a gory sight, with legs and ankles streaming. The first day we got in rather a panic about all this, but it was wonderful how soon we began to take it all for granted like the porters and the animals. No harm is done in the long run, though I would hate to have to sleep out in the wet grass in the leech season. That is another thing the men have to contend with in some parts of the Burma front.

We have been sitting out watching some birds catching insects in the air. It was most fascinating. We finally located the source of supply under the wood of the veranda. These flying ants were hatching out there and attempting to fly away. Before the majority found their wings, they were set upon by huge black ants, who ate them alive or carried them off to their nest. Those who managed to fly were immediately caught by the birds, so only about half of one per cent survived. That is just as well as they breed white ants eventually and they eat everything except metal.

This appears to be quite a bloodthirsty place, what with ant battles and leeches.

As usual we have had a great washing of wet things and have brought in two clothes horses festooned with garments. The two new porters arrived late and very tired.

SONG – 4,500 ft
Sunday 9 July 1944 (12 miles)

We had a good view this morning from Temi bungalow, looking towards the Natu La and Jelap La, the two gateways into Tibet. All the peaks were snow covered. The early part of the march was a rather rough descent of seven miles to the river Tista, where we crossed by a well-constructed bridge. It was a swiftly flowing river, the colour of cement. We passed through a very dirty bazaar the other side where, according to the book, was "a pleasant rest house for tiffin". This we considered a very dirty hut and passed on. It was rather like the family looking for a suitable picnic spot, always expecting better things around the next corner and then feeling certain the last place would have been better.

Eventually we ate our lunch on some rather uncomfortable stones. Ila was with us but the others had waited in the bazaar. The pony was a great asset and the rest of us looked with rather envious eyes on Jessie and her white steed. The rest of the way was a pretty steep and rough climb of five miles and very hot. The sweat fairly poured off. We rested every hour for ten minutes and were more than thankful to reach the bungalow. This is very pretty and the garden is gay with flowers. It is dry today so we have no leeches. On arrival we just lay on the grass without any thought of insects. The word 'tea', however, brought us flying in to quench our thirst.

Tonight we have just finished a great council of war as to our future plans. We had meant to go up the east branch of the Tista over the Sebu La and down the west branch, but that means dividing the party as the women porters and pony cannot cross the Sebu La. We think it is better to stick together and those that feel inclined can tackle the Sebu La when we reach Thangu.

The two new porters were very late again. We are sending them back from Gantok and hope to get others there. They would never last out the trip. They are not lazy, but just not strong enough. We have also to send Chitty back as his owner cannot spare him any longer. I don't expect we will get as sturdy a beast in Gantock.

GANTOK – 5,800 ft
Monday 10 July 1944 (15 miles)

Left Song 8.00 a.m. Glorious walk through woods and past innumerable waterfalls. The weather was fine and we had some grand views, the best being of the ridge of mountains guarding Tibet – they rise to 19,000 ft, and the two passes, Natu La and Jelap La (14,000 ft) were visible. These are the trade routes to Tibet and to China.

All along, the hillsides were terraced with paddy fields, the young plants being a solid mass of very bright green. At increasingly frequent intervals young rivers crossed our path.

We passed the Monastery of Rumtek, which I thought disappointing after the one I visited on my own at Rimbick in 1942. The lamas at this one were wanting bakshish all the time. We eventually reached the River Rongni, a fine rushing torrent with boulders beside it. We sat there and had some tea, Bernard disgracing himself by dropping one of the four mugs into the torrent. I lay for a while on a lovely flat rock and daydreamed. There is such a fascination lying by running water. I felt I might have been in Glen Rosa (Arran), as long as I kept my eyes shut.

The five mile climb up to Gantok was not pleasant. It was very hot, and the bridle path of short cuts was just a solid slog. Jessie and Stanley kept to the road with the pony and had a very tiring time. Bernard and I went on ahead as we were a bit concerned about the dak bungalow accommodation; there was some doubt as to passes too. Eventually we reached Gantok, the capital of Sikkim. The bazaar had an entrance with a gatehouse over it. We met all manner of strange-looking people, from dirty-looking muleteers with very sad-looking mules, many with huge sores on their backs, and other porters distinguished by odd pieces of European clothes from past expeditions and by much chat with our men, to some very magnificent Tibetan men, in long purple coats slung up at the waist and showing gorgeous blue shirts below, breeches and high boots with fur lining.

On arrival we found the place full, but our lives were saved by a very ancient and toothless Chaukidar who gave us a great welcome and seats on his back doorstep. He brought us ice water, of which we drank pints. Then the 'cake man' appeared, carrying on his head a small tin trunk, inside which cakes and bread were to be found. We looked in and bought rolls and small cakes, and this took the edge off our rather ravenous appetites. A very smart bearer came and looked at us, rather horrified at a 'Sahib and Memsahib' sitting on the doorstep in this fashion. As a result we were asked in to tea and found ourselves entertained by a Colonel and Mrs Hislop. He was an Indian medical superintendent (I.M.S) and surgeon in Tibet. He had some very interesting stories to tell, but she was so busy trying to impress us with what a grand lady she was. Needless to say she did not get far. They were both going to dinner with the Maharaja, their farewell visit on retiring after many years. They both disappeared to change, and imagine our amusement when she returned in a long dinner gown such as is seen in London. I nearly laughed outright. In Gantok with no roads or hardly any, and what rain there was that night!

After endless chits to and fro, a note came telling us to go to one of the bungalows where a wireless operator lived in two rooms, leaving the other half of two rooms for the broadcasting station. One of these he was asked to clear for us to sleep in. We were more than delighted, when we had begun to imagine ourselves camping out in the garden in the rain. We all helped clear and finally all the etceteras, including gramophone records, were stowed to one side and a trestle table pulled to the middle.

The two porters arrived very late again. They are glad we are sending them back; they look all in.

Here we are now, all four of us; there is just room to climb out of one's sleeping bag without standing on the next man or woman! I don't know how hard we will find the floor.

The porters are like sardines in a sort of corridor. It can't be very pleasant but there is much laughter, so they must be happy. The room off our 'bedroom' is almost filled with transmitters; the small space left over has made a very good dressing room. If only all our friends could have a bird's eye view of the four of us, I think it would give them all a good laugh. A week or more ago we wouldn't have believed it possible.

DICKCHU – 2,150 ft
Tuesday, 11 July 1944 (13 miles)

A most varied and eventful day.

We slept well in our rather odd surroundings. We were so tired we found the wooden floor almost soft. How I laughed to myself when I woke and looked at our little party all so cosily tucked up round the broadcasting apparatus. Gylgen and Sona were in early to call us and soon there was great activity of washing and dressing and then the bedding rolls to be disposed of and the table put ready. We consumed a huge breakfast of porridge, bacon, eggs, tomatoes, toast and jam.

Mr Baker started his broadcast at 8.00 a.m. so we had to be out of the way by then. We wondered if the Tibetans would hear the expedition waking as an alternative programme!

There was great activity on the veranda amongst the porters. Our own men set off early as they wanted to get well ahead. The syce and Chitty were paid off and sent back to Namchi. We were sorry to see such a fine sturdy pony go, especially when we saw the replacements. Goodness, the ponies looked in poor shape, except one. He was loaded with the two bedding rolls belonging to J & B. They have a small wooden saddle with two bars each side to which the loads are tied. The other three ponies were saddled in the same way, two with odd coats etc. thrown over for riding purposes. They looked very uncomfortable.

Ila was to wait for us on the Penlong La for lunch and he made a start with the syce and ponies.

The two spare porters were paid off and sent back to Darjeeling with a note to Mr Kydd. We gave them some bakshish and they seemed very grateful. They limped off down the hill. Gylgen went to the bazaar and then joined us at the residency. This was in lovely grounds.

We found the small office and soon realised the magnitude of the task before us – officialdom and red tape. The obstacles and complications mounted every minute but made us all the more determined to stick to our plan. The Resident, Sir Basil Gould, had gone to Darjeeling to avoid large numbers of Chinese staying in his house en route for Tibet. Every corner in Gantok was filled with various attendants in the Mission. This was very unfortunate for us as we were left to deal with some head clerk. He thought we might leave the next day, with luck! Our porters were now well on their way to Dickchu, 14 miles away! After much diplomacy etc. we had the passes on the understanding that if the Maharaja objected to our route we would return on a message reaching us. At last we emerged with the passes – victorious – but no one seemed to know where we would find the keys to the club huts. I was beginning to have a horrible feeling that I should have applied for them in Calcutta; as time went on I was more and more certain.

J, B & S walked on and I went back to find the State Engineer for the keys. He wasn't in and I had a great chase all over for him. B joined me after a while and we were soon rewarded by finding the said engineer, an elderly Sikh and a most charming person – so different from the officials we had encountered earlier in the day. He had the keys and handed them over, so my worst fears were not realised. With great enthusiasm we stepped out to catch up the others, expecting to make good time on this easy path, mostly downhill.

We met J & S and then continued up to Penlong La (6,300 ft). It grew colder and we sheltered the other side of the pass, a narrow path between high rock. Here we ate our lunch, rather hastily, as the rain started and the leeches came to join us.

The way down soon became rough and the rain came in buckets. In between whiles we had the most magnificent views of the river Dickchu hundreds of feet below in a gorge, and all the valleys with very steep sides and range upon range of mountains folding into one another and disappearing in the clouds.

Water poured down the mountain sides and we crossed several quite large rivers by most precarious bridges, some just a couple of logs thrown across. Some we just waded through, and often being in part of a young waterfall and quite deep, we were in over the knees.

Our next obstacle was a landslide which had happened the day before and a detour had to be made. It was about half a mile in width. We followed the tracks made by feet of the local inhabitants and passers-by. The little syce did good work on ahead improving the road with the ice axe. The ponies were very clever at picking their way over these bad bits.

In one place the path led along a kind of shelf in the cliff, made of branches of trees, lime and mud. It moved oddly as we walked over. The syce went behind each pony in turn, holding on by its tail. This served to have a very good moral effect on the ponies! A little further on, just as we were thinking of that cup of tea and a log fire and how grand it was to have the porters so many hours ahead to have everything ready for us, we met our real obstacle. B and I were ahead and to our amazement we saw the porters sitting with their loads in a cave saying we could get no further. We hurried on and soon found the reason. There had been another landslide in and over a waterfall. The path led through the torrent, with water tumbling down above and a drop of hundreds of feet below. Things did look bad, but Gylgen had got through and gone ahead to the bungalow, so we must too.

With the aid of a local man and two porters with sticks, we found a way and finally, the four of us holding hands, we made it. The current was terrific and it was over our knees, but there was a flat bit, with boulders, so we could ford it a few feet from the edge.

B & I decided to wait and see the porters over, even if we could be of no help. The men came over easily carrying their heavy loads. Two stood in the middle with sticks and gave a hand. Gylgen arrived at that point and at once went for the women, who came down from the cave with their loads. He in turn carried all four loads himself and then he and these other two helped the women over. They had to tuck their long skirts up round their waists.

B tried to help and stood down by the water, but Gylgen told him to move, as another fall might come at any minute. They were so pleased that we had stayed to see them over and we saw that we had a fine team of men who were really reliable in an emergency. They would never let us down.

Cheerful but wet and cold and with many leeches we reached the bungalow at 6.30 p.m.

These men and women are really incredible, they must have been just as weary or more so than we and yet all of them dash round seeing to our comforts, making up the beds, tea and hot water and preparing dinner before sitting down to having their meal. They sleep in a kind of hall, all together, each rolled in his blanket.

The bungalow is very pretty and has a large veranda where we had tea, looking on to the garden with flowers and to the river below. We set off for bed even earlier than usual and left the room festooned with clothes to dry.

The ponies arrived about an hour later. Ila had carried the bedding rolls over and a local man had helped the syce with the ponies.

SINGHIK – 4,600 ft
Wednesday, 12 July 1944 (10 miles)

I had a busy time before we set out. Three of the ponies have very bad sores on their backs, one a huge deep thing on his withers; the smell from them is really foul. We have Dettol with us and I washed them with that and dressed them with the same, putting a large sling to cover the whole of them and then making holes in the various blankets under the saddle. The syce doesn't seem to mind me interfering. One of them seems horribly weak, but there is no need for him to carry anything. We are paying for three, one pack and two riding.

We finally set off at 9.35 after breakfast on the veranda. It was lovely.

We followed close beside the bank of the Tista and in some parts it was quite a scramble with landslides caused by the waterfalls. Some local men were busy mending one part and busy making a path. One old worthy told us he had heard we were coming and hastened to have the road open. He asked us where we were going and was very thrilled on hearing we hoped to reach Sebu La; he had been there in his youth.

We passed a bridge consisting of three long pieces of bamboo about 4 inches in diameter slung by strips of bamboo from two wire cables – a very frail looking affair, and we were rather glad we could pass it by. A few miles further we crossed the Rongrong by a suspension bridge of 250 ft long by about 250 ft high. It was a very well constructed affair. We picnicked here and sat awhile and admired the rushing torrent in the gorge below.

Our way led up from here and it was at first hot, but soon we found the cooler mountain air. The path was high above the river, with the mountains rising steeply and numerous waterfalls cascading down through the trees and over rocks like some beautiful white lace curtain.

We passed Mangan, a little village, and found the now familiar boxes and bedding rolls parked on a wall. The porters were having tea. The owner of the ponies made himself known and wanted us to take all four ponies. However, we were firm about that and also told him of the shocking state of their backs. He promised to change the other two saddles for riding ones.

About a mile from the bungalow we found a magnificent view, looking up the Talung gorge. The river winds like a snake hundreds of feet below.

The path was a delight, wandering through woods bright with butterflies of the most glorious colours. The day was dry and sunny, so we had no leeches to worry us. We reached the bungalow about teatime and soon we were *munching* pancakes.

This is a glorious place, the prettiest bungalow we have seen. The view on a clear day is said to be the finest in Sikkim. We looked with B's glasses up the Talung gorge; the mountains fold in from each side, but the highest peaks were hidden by mist. Kanchenjunga is 25 miles away and rises at the head of this valley.

We saw the glaciers on Pandim, and the drifting cloud revealed numerous peaks and ridges, including Simva, and just about sunset the top of Kanchenjunga incredibly far above the clouds.

CHUNGTHANG – 5,600 ft
Thursday, 13 July 1944 (13 miles)

Woke early, about 6.00 a.m., and looked towards Kanchenjunga from my bed, but there was nothing but mist. Later, we saw the top of Kanchenjunga high above the valley, the supreme monarch standing on a throne of cloud. The view was of the eastern face, showing a sharp ridge and terrific snow and ice slopes. All the other peaks were covered.

We left at 9 am, first dealing with the ponies. Two of them have very bad sores on their backs. The little syce was quite helpful and we fixed the saddles as best we could. They seem much happier today, though the pack horse got a bit weary and just lay down, complete with bedding rolls. However, he soon jumped up when the syce chased him. I think they should benefit by their stay with us, five days with no work and us paying for it!

Our way led up and down through woods and past innumerable waterfalls and two landslides. One was very recent, and the syce and a local helper moved stones to make it better for the ponies. The ponies were then unloaded and they got over with a man at the head and the syce hanging on to the tail. The ponies really are wonderful the way they pick their way over these stones and waterfalls. Ila carried the loads over.

We had lunch by a waterfall. It was a magnificent sight. The water tumbled down in great cataracts over a distance of 250 ft. We crossed by a rather delicate wooden bridge. The ponies and all the porters crossing in a long line made a very impressive sight. I must try to get a photo on the way back. We fed by the water's edge; afterwards I climbed up to a perch on a rock and just lay there and revelled in it. I think I could have remained there for hours.

I must try to climb up to the pool below the upper fall next time. The others went on and left me to follow when I had come out of my daydreaming, but the faithful Ila wasn't going to have me forgotten. He asked Bernard if I was coming and he replied I would follow in my own good time, but that wasn't good enough. He said he would wait or else Bernard must. We passed over two other falls by little bridges, and the river below was running through solid rock. We were following up the Tista river, and the path was a contour one high above. At intervals there were glorious views up and down the valleys.

The leeches today were worse than at any time, they just hung on in dozens. I was wearing shoes instead of boots and puttees as I had strained the tendon on my left heel and could not wear boots. I think they must be in the water, as every time I was over the ankles in water I found a fresh bunch on my socks. The natives don't seem to worry much and just let them have their fill and then drop off, leaving their legs and feet streaming with blood.

There was much laughter when we passed a black and white cow sitting in the middle of the path and I stopped to have a few words with it and at the same time trying to pull some of the leeches off. The cow was sitting on top of armies of them. My efforts were abandoned when Peter the pony butted me in the back and ordered me to proceed.

The last part of the trek was very wet. The scenery was rather mild and we passed some more landslides. The river was the colour of liquid cement, presumably from a fall higher up, as when we reached the bungalow, by the junction of the two tributaries the Lachen, and the Lachung, the former was muddy colour while the latter was crystal clear.

We crossed the Lachen by iron bridge. From here in bygone days condemned criminals were flung into the boiling torrent to see if they were guilty. The oldest inhabitants are said to remember it still happening.

Tonight is much cooler and I am glad of my cashmere twin set. We have fed as usual very well. Gylgan is full of surprises. We had very fine dhal soup, bully beef stew with all manner of vegetables, and peaches and custard, ending with a nightcap of cocoa.

In spite of all this I think we are all losing weight but are getting so fit at the same time. To think it is just a week since we started. Time doesn't seem to count out here and the war just doesn't exist.

LACHEN – 8,800 ft
Friday 14 July 1944 (13 miles)

Today was the best yet, just a series of unforgettable sights. We started at 8.30 a.m. with Jessie on the pony after the usual ceremony of dressing its back.

The early part of the march was up and down gentle slopes through thick woods and still with many waterfalls. The Lachen became gradually less and less cement like until we passed another tributary, which seemed to be the source of the trouble – there had been quite a recent slide there. We had quite a chat with a dear old man who was busily digging a path for us out of the cliff. The local inhabitants have been most helpful all the way.

We stopped for a while in a beautiful meadow where we had coffee. Bernard and I arrived first and I put in the time by being stung by a wasp. Jessie arrived on her steed accompanied by two magnificent specimens. They looked like the wicked pirates, dressed with Tibetan coats hanging from the waist and one with a ragged shirt and the other with nothing but his load wrapped in a plaid slung over his shoulder. Both had old balaclava helmets crowning their untidy heads with hair plaited and wound round their heads. Jessie had scratched her leg on a buckle of the saddle and I was about to put some elastoplast on. Both men and syce were very interested and after seeing B hold one end of the plaster for me to cut, one man held on to the piece of gauze I was cutting, with his glorious grubby hands, and so the dressing was completed with full aseptic precautions. Later in the day the said elastoplast fell off; the same man picked it up and put it on Jessie again, but as it didn't stick he first blew on it and finally licked it to help matters on!

We lunched as yesterday by the most glorious waterfall, tumbling from a great height. It got suddenly much cooler and we were very glad of jackets and hot coffee. I noticed the construction of the bridge this time.

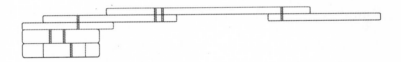

It was quite a solid one. Later we crossed a suspension bridge over the Lachen. It was quite an experience as numerous planks were missing and the whole thing seemed most insecure. The pack pony refused it till the syce and Gylgen had put more planks in the holes.

After this we started to climb, and B & I were on in front of Jessie, and Stanley away ahead of us. The scenery grew grander every minute and after crossing more falls the path rose steeply through pine woods until we reached Alpine country. Suddenly we came out in the open amongst numerous flowers, forget-me-

131

nots, marguerites, Michaelmas daisies, lavender, rosemary and irises. The view was of steep mountains all around, all pine clad and the river rushing down the sides to 1,000 ft. below. B & I were on ahead and we sat at this point and waited and just drank in the grandeur. A little further on we came to a wide Swiss-like meadow, with pine trees at intervals.

There was another steep climb and so up to Lachen and the bungalow. The village is rather attractive, rather like pictures of Switzerland. It is much colder and we have much appreciated a large log fire. Once again Gylgen gave us a magnificent dinner of chicken and pancakes for tea.

THANGU – 12,800 ft
Saturday, 15 July (13 miles)

We had an interesting time looking through the book at all the people who had stayed at Lachen.

The Everest parties had been, and a German expedition in 1939, complete with their own rubber stamp. Apparently they were picked up by plane in Tibet and escaped just as War broke out. Smythe had been on his way to the Zenu glacier in 1942.

We left about 8.30 a.m. and started with a lovely walk through pine woods with the River Lachen always near at hand. The mountains around were a grand sight, but very little snow to be seen.

A suspension bridge crossed the Zenu River, and at the other side there was a little path leading west up the river towards the glacier. Later the path climbed very steeply and was very rough. Parts of it had fallen away with the recent rains and had been repaired again. Every now and then there were fine cascades of water tumbling down the perpendicular cliffs on the other side of the Lachen. In spite of the steepness, shrubs and pine trees were growing.

The rain descended just as we were looking for a nice spot for lunch and it was getting pretty cold. However, Ila insisted that we went on a bit to a village, Tanum Samdong by name. There we finally came to rest in the shelter of the wall of a small house. We sat on logs of wood, Bernard choosing the pig trough. We ate our sandwiches, much to the amusement and interest of several families who stood round us. An old lady was spinning wool from a bundle round her wrist. She just pulled and twisted it and then spun it round a wooden spindle. We gave the children some raisins and they were highly delighted.

A little later we passed a camp of Tibetans. It was a rather desolate strip of land with a stony pathway. Looking back it reminded me of a scene from *Macbeth*, with Jessie, a hooded figure on her pony, and the pack pony and porters with their loads winding their way across. After walking up another steeply wooded river valley we sighted the bungalow high up on the side of a hill between two rivers, the Lachen and Lasha Chu. The valleys opened out below into a delightful spot. The rivers rushed over boulders, turning and twisting, rather like parts of Glen Rosa. The ground each side was boulder strewn and thick with flowers and shrubs and lovely grass. We lay there for a while before scrambling up to the bungalow. Here and there were patches of potatoes, well fenced in with branches of trees – it seemed to be the only crop.

The bungalow is comfortable and the cleanest we have met. The Chaukidar is quite a character, a Tibetan with a long plait and his gown. This is rather like a long dressing gown done up Chinese style down the side, the whole hitched up round the hips with a scarf. The coat is open about 9–12 inches up each side at the bottom.

We have had another fine meal and are thoroughly enjoying a huge log fire.

THANGU – 13,000 ft
Sunday, 16 July, 1944

I am writing this by the light of the hurricane lamp and beside a huge log fire. It really is very cold. Last night I slept inside my Jaeger sleeping bag with two more blankets on top.

I slept in my Viyella pyjamas plus a wool vest and a long pair of bed socks.

This has been a complete day of rest, except for Stanley who climbed about 1,000 ft. up a grassy hill behind the bungalow. The rest of us just lazed and pottered. It was a great field day of drying and airing our belongings. Our bedding rolls have been soaked through nearly every day and never dried off. The grass around was strewn with every article we possessed. The porters were at it first thing in the morning. They have been busy washing and airing their things and lying in the sun. They have had a pretty busy trip so far.

The flowers here are really wonderful, but I don't know many of their names. We have seen blue poppies and lots of marigolds and yellow polyanthus on very long stalks. It is such a joy to be able to lie on the grass and not be eaten by any strange pest. There are fine mountain views all round and quite a bit of snow on the tops. The Lanak La is to be seen due west and another just south of it.

I washed my hair and lay out in the sun drying it all morning. It was glorious. Two yaks walked up, a black and a white one: what strange beasts they are. My legs are badly burnt from the sun this morning, and I am busy treating them. Some of us are feeling the height a bit, Bernard and I having our tummies affected still. I hope they settle down before tomorrow. We are rather living on eggs, cheese and Klim.

The porters are very thrilled about the possibility of reaching the Sebu La – 17,600 ft. Gylgen, our sirdar, has been several times; he is a grand fellow. We read his book of chits given by the Himalayan Club. He has done very interesting treks and also been on Everest and Kanchenjunga. He was Shipton's personal porter and is very proud of the fact.

Gylgen has chosen the rest of the party. They are Dawa Tundup, who has done it before several times, and Sona Pemba Sherpa – he is the lad who was with me in '42, a wonderful, cheerful little person. He waits the table in the bungalows and does it with great style, wearing his balaclava helmet all the time and his prayer beads round his wrist. He is an enthusiastic Buddhist.

He carries a load of about 80 lb and always is one of the first to arrive. He has been over the pass carrying 85 lb. Two others complete the party: Stanley's bedding roll porter and Pemba Nuvwu, both very good lads.

Bed calls, we have to be very early tomorrow and do hope the weather holds.

CLUB HUT – 16,000 ft
Monday, 17 July, 1944 (8 miles)

We were off this morning at 7.00 a.m., leaving Jessie mid the rest of the porters, who gave us quite a send off. The women were a trifle dismal, and then it was pointed out that a special fire had been lit beside the prayer flags to ask the gods for our safe return.

A prayer flag is a piece of cotton varying in size from a few inches to several feet in length. On these are printed prayers and they are attached to long poles and erected anywhere, but especially near monasteries.

The small ones are tied onto all odd places, onto bridges and on cairns. They give great credit to the owner as those prayers are being said continually for their benefit. With all this we began to think we were starting quite an expedition.

Our way led up a very steep path by a river and then we turned into a fine valley. The flowers were really an incredible sight. Stanley described it as the Chelsea Flower Show x 100. Lots of rock plants which we rear with difficulty, just growing in profusion. Amongst them all was the edelweiss.

We wandered on beside the river and at one point had to cross where it was quite deep. The porters had already crossed with their loads and three of them returned for us. Gylgen approached me and told me to jump up, so off I went in great style pick-a-back, clasping Gylgen round the neck. It was knee deep most of the way.

We stopped for some coffee out of our flasks and Gylgen offered us some yak cream he had bought. It was in a section of a bamboo stem. It tasted horribly sour.

A little later we saw a yak herd slowly coming down the hillside. They looked like beetles in the distance. Soon we were all amongst them and what strange beasts. They are very short legged and have a cloven hoof, altogether not unlike a cow. Their hair is very long, about 12 inches, and their tails are more like those of Shetland ponies. They grunt rather like a pig. They are only found above 10,000 ft, and they give milk and carry heavy loads over mountain trails. The dried dung also provides fuel. There were pack ponies and mules also in the party and many women and children. They were all Tibetan. They salaamed us politely and we all walked on together. One of the senior men had a fine dagger hanging from his waist and. I cast covetous eyes at it and then asked Sona to tell him I wanted it and for how much. He gladly gave it, and all for the cost of Rs. 5. The porters say it is a good one and I was very lucky to get it.

Soon we came to a sheltered spot by the river, and at the foot of the mountain here was the Himalayan club hut, our destination for today.

The Tibetans pitched their camp, consisting of two tents. There were already stones piled to a height of about one foot in three circles of about the size of a ball tent. Inside these they put up a square tent, rather marquee-like with pole at each corner and across the top. They fixed guys in the usual way and in no time smoke was rising from all parts of the tent. However, it did not seem to worry them.

The ponies and mules were unsaddled and left to graze, and we were amazed to see in what perfect condition they were – fat and well cared for and no sores. In India that is almost a miracle.

The children were very curious and came up to us as we walked about. I had a pocketful of boiled sweets and gave them some, and they were highly delighted after I demonstrated what was to be done with them. The coloured paper was carefully preserved. There were quite a few small babies too, slung up on the children's backs in shawls.

We watched them cutting the wool from a yak which protested violently. They tied its two fore feet together and to its horns, but even so it capered about as if it was a rodeo performance.

Later in the evening the milking began and there was a wild chase to catch all the little ones and tether them to a long rope. This took some time and then they tied. the fore feet and milked the yaks.

They seemed a very happy contented. people and very fit too. I think they just move about a few miles every few days. They made no attempt to beg which was a wonderful thing after India.

Our hut is very cosy except for the smoke. We are all sitting with eyes streaming. It is an iron stove that burns anything. The smoke should go up the chimney but instead it pours out everywhere. It will be three kippers that will be found in the morning.

The hut is in two rooms, one for the kitchen occupying one-third of the space, with the other two-thirds taken up by a living and sleeping room. The walls of this last are lined with charpois [rope beds], five in all, and in the middle is a table and two chairs. There is a loft above each room for further sleeping accommodation. Thank goodness we didn't have to rely on breaking down the door as it is a most solid construction, double doors and windows and a great Yale padlock. There is always enough wood left to start off the next comer. The club maintains this and another hut the other side of the pass and all wanderers can use it.

I do wish we had longer; really we should have had several days doing climbs from Thangu and then on here and more scrambles up the valleys round about. There are no end of little expeditions possible either daily or else for several days, taking a tent. In eleven days we have come from sea level and only for the last four have we been over 8,000 ft. It isn't nearly enough time for acclimatisation for heights. Stanley has been all right except for some headache and a bit of

139

depression. He gets very short of breath easily but soon recovers after a rest. Bernard and I have had really bad stomach upsets and have had to live on Klim and cheese and eggs. Today I didn't feel like eating at all, much to Gylgen's distress. At this rate he must wonder if he will ever get us up the pass. He and Dawa Tundup are so enthusiastic. I hope we don't disappoint them, but we have no idea how we will react at even greater heights.

THANGU

Tuesday, 18 July, 1944

Sitting beside a big log fire, having had a good meal, it seems rather unbelievable that we have been up the Sebu La (17,600 ft) and back to the hut and on here. Still, let me begin at the beginning. I personally felt so queer last night I had almost made up my mind to go back to the bungalow with the other three porters as the likelihood of me getting up was almost nil. Apparently we had all felt the same but said nothing.

It was terribly cold last night and we slept with every available bit of clothing. I had a woollen vest and Bernard's long men's woollen pants, three pullovers, and over that Viyella pyjamas and long operation woollen stockings to my thighs. The next layer was a cashmere blanket and then inside my Jaeger sleeping bag. By the time I had thawed I felt just comfortable.

In desperation we let the fire go out and had my window open and so got rid of the smoke. I slept pretty well and really felt better this morning but the other two had little sleep and Bernard a splitting headache.

Gylgen came in about 5.30 a.m. and peered at us, enquiring rather doubtfully for Memsahib's well-being. I had spent most of the afternoon and evening in my sleeping bag and had not been exactly bubbling over with the joy of spring. Gylgen and Sona first brought us tea and finally our breakfast of porridge and scrambled eggs in bed. After more very sweet tea we began to thaw and show a little more interest in life and the Sebu La in particular.

Eventually at 7.45 a.m. we set off on the great adventure. Our route lay beside the stream for a while and then a steep scramble up rocks, very like that up to all the lochans on the Cuillins. It was hard going but I found I was feeling fine and not very breathless. This continued until we reached the snow field, about 500 ft below the top, then the fun began. We thought of Mr Kydd laughing at me requesting an ice axe and that we had nailed boots. Without both, this last part would have been quite impossible.

At first Dawa Tundup led, followed by Bernard and Stanley with Gylgen bringing up the rear. The first bit was thin ice and so slippery. I found myself thinking of all the things George had always tried to drum into me. They stood me in good stead too. Tundup was busy cutting steps and it must have been hard work, plus carrying a rucksack of about 40 lb. When we got on to the snow it was easier as there was little danger of us slipping. Gylgen moved up to the front and he and Tundup roped in case of crevasses. The snow was very soft and we sank nearly to our waists at times. The other two crossed this bad bit without encountering the crevasse and we followed very slowly. We were all feeling the height by now. Stanley was very breathless, Bernard had a terrific headache and was a bad colour, and I had a headache to a lesser degree. I think we all felt a bit sick. It turned out afterwards that both Bernard and I had had amoebic dysentery throughout the trek, so that accounted for most of our troubles.

Gylgen and Tundup waited on an outcrop of rock just below the summit. When we reached them they waved to me to go on: they wanted the Memsahib to be the first one up. After a few minutes we were on the summit and glad to sink down on to a rock. We had made it, and it was a good feeling in spite of our physical discomforts.

We were on the pass between the valleys of the Lachen and Lachung to the west and east; north rose Kanchenjunga, a magnificent peak of 22,700 ft. The top was rather flat with a covering of snow like a tablecloth. The snow and ice hanging from the precipices were like a fine lace curtain. To the south rose Chombu (21,000 ft), also unclimbed. This was in the mist, but we had seen it the day before on our way to the hut. The ridges leading to these two mountains spring from the pass. We were sitting on an almost knife-like edge, just like the ridges of the Black Cuillins. Looking down to the Lachung valley was completely different to the side we had climbed up. It was very rough and stony but with no snow. About 500 ft below there were some lakes and many possible camping places. There was a ledge just below the summit where Gylgen said he had camped. Beyond the Lachung valley rose the ridge dividing Tibet from Sikkim mountains rising to 20,000 ft, ten miles away.

Both these porters had been over the pass on several occasions and each time they added more stones to their particular cairn.

There was quite a ceremony about it. They were collecting up the stones and arranging them all pointing skywards, singing Buddhist chants and prayers all the time! They topped the cairn with little prayer flags they had brought with them and after a final prayer they came and sat. I told them I wanted to put a stone on a cairn too, not being sure if my stone could go on their cairn. They were most insistent that I should add it to theirs and helped me select a suitable one and place it the right way up.

These two were a grand pair. There was such a feeling of comradeship amongst us all. They were so proud that we had reached our goal without mishap. Gylgen had been up here with Mr and Mrs Case, my friends in Calcutta who belong to the Himalayan Club. He was very pleased that I knew them.

After half an hour, about 1.00 p.m., we started on our way down again. We took some photos, but due to my carelessness the first four were spoilt. The camera, a box one, had accidentally been set to time instead of instant. Only one came out of four of us going down the snow field. It was grand going down, I glissaded most of the way. It was an easy matter scrambling down the boulders and once down by the river we stopped for some tiffin, we were feeling almost hungry. The five of us, including Gylgen and Dawa Tundup, tucked into cocoa, cheese and hard boiled eggs. That is another thing that is such a relief from the Indian way. These fellows have a much simpler religion, and food doesn't enter into it.

We missed the hut and kept on the other side of the river. We were all wishing we could just spend the night in the hut and have a good sleep instead of plodding on back to Thangu. If it hadn't been for Jessie we should have done; a double march was far too much at that height when we were not acclimatised. Gylgen hurried on at a good pace to organise the tea and supper.

We followed somewhat slowly. It was very cold and I was very thankful for Mother's big white scarf over my head and ears.

It was a glorious walk back through this high Alpine valley and beside the river babbling over boulders like every highland stream. It really was a paradise. I would love to spend days there roaming round. At the time we were in no shape to appreciate anything, just mechanically plodding on. Dawa Tundup was so concerned about us as he sensed we weren't feeling too good.

After what seemed an age we arrived back at the bungalow to receive a great welcome from Jessie and all the porters. After a stiff dose of the never failing aspirin and gallons of hot tea, drunk round a roaring log fire, we felt completely new beings. This was followed by a hot bath and we were quite ready for our supper of roast chicken and peaches followed by the inevitable half pint of cocoa.

LACHEN

Wednesday, 19 July 1944

We were later starting this morning and first took a photo of the entire party, plus the Chaukidar and ponies. The smallest pony was in a shocking state, a huge new sore on its back and it just looked ready to lie down and die. The syce must have hired it out while we were up the mountain. I was furious with him though the language was rather a problem as he only spoke the local dialect. I made him carry all the oddments including the saddle and let the pony go without anything.

I dressed the wound with Dettol and fixed a couple of triangular bandages round his middle. They must all think I am quite daft. There were odd comments from passers-by regarding the bandages!

The weather was still showery, but not so bad as going up. We had to make a detour on account of a further landslide and the path was rather precarious in parts. However, with the syce holding on to the ponies' tails in turn, the bad parts were negotiated.

We had lunch in a meadow and fed on wild strawberries. Our lunch usually consisted of hard boiled eggs, cheese, marmite and a ration biscuit. We were at Lachen bungalow in good time.

CHUNGTHANG
Thursday, 20 July 1944

A glorious day. It was sunny and at first we wandered, lingering in the meadows amongst wild flowers in profusion. We sat awhile on the crest of the hill looking down to the valleys and pine clad hills; what a view to be remembered. I felt I wanted to stay just there in the mountains and not go back to the hot steamy plains. We would have more fine views, but this was the last of open hillside.

Eventually I tore myself away and we hurried down the path, through pine woods and over rivers and falls. We passed a caravan of yaks, all beautifully groomed, with long shiny coats. They were carrying loads of wood.

We met the others by the rickety bridge. It was still awaiting repair with planks all ready.

We found a good place to picnic, mostly in a river, each sitting on our own rock. It was handy for washing the dried fruit. Watercress was growing in abundance and within easy reach for adding to our menu.

We reached Chungthang about 3.00 p.m. and reviewed the stores. We had left a box of provisions behind. We had more than enough.

DICKCHU
Friday, 21 July 1944

We had some coffee by a waterfall, where the path led over boulders and then across a bridge of logs. I tried to take a photo of the entire party crossing, but the one pony with the bad back slipped and nearly fell down the mountain. The syce ran and caught him by the tail and all was well. I took the rest of the party crossing, pack pony and porters.

B & I went on ahead and reached the bungalow about 2.00 p.m. We had previously stopped for a bite of lunch, standing in the path: the leeches were too bad.

Just before getting in we met some men improving the path over a boulder-strewn landslide and amongst them the owner of the ponies. We told him to come to the bungalow and he could have the ponies. He arrived and we told him of the bad condition of one pony which we were quite certain the syce had hired out during our absence in the mountains. He agreed to our surprise that we should only pay for two, when he realised it added to Rs. 110. I suppose he never imagined such a lump sum. Not only was he profuse in his thanks, but gave us a fine present of new laid eggs. He left us with great instructions as to how he was to treat his ponies in future.

DICKCHU
Saturday, 22 July 1944

I had my bed by the window and woke at dawn to see just the peak of Kanchenjunga visible high above the clouds. I woke Jessie and then later I woke to see the whole range visible, still above the clouds. The snow looked like pure gold – a throne in the skies.

It was a very easy march, all downhill, but getting sticky and with more leeches. We passed through Mangan and saw our late syce busy with pestle and mortar, grinding corn. He seemed pleased to see us.

We reached the bungalow in good time, and that was fortunate. As we sat having tea Gylgen came and said another sahib and memsahib were coming. We knew they could not have booked, so decided to leave them the veranda. Porters dribbled in, and finally a bearer in long coat and turban, carrying an umbrella. The sahib and memsahib next appeared. He was a British M.O. and was clad in uniform and chapplies (sort of sandals with no backs). She was Indian, also an M.O. and in uniform, complete with peaked cap, stockings and neat shoes with one and half inch high heel – there was no sign of travel, mud or dust, and they had just come over the path where we had crossed innumerable waterfalls and landslides! Later a very well-kept pony arrived; presumably she had ridden. They installed themselves on the veranda, each having a bedding roll and large suitcase, revealing piles of clean, starched shirts, etc.!

I repaired to bath and to my amazement heard strains of a symphony concert. I really thought I must be going queer. On emerging I found the source of music – a gramophone and two big boxes of records! Later they had their meal, in every instance giving their instructions for requirements to the bearer, who in turn conveyed them to the cook, sirdar, who gloried in the name of Underwear. The said porter looked as if he could gladly murder this Bengali bearer with the superior manner. I expect they all got equal with him

148

by the time the trip was out, especially in fording any passing waterfalls.

Their provisions included numerous bottles of refreshment, set out like a West End cocktail bar.

We chatted to them and found it had been dry and they had met no leeches and seen no landslides or waterfalls more than a few inches deep.

B & I went for a scramble up the Dickchu gorge. It was almost like a beach – little sandy bays surrounded by rocks.

We fed on chicken again, a very fine meal.

GANTOK
Sunday, 23 July 1944

A long and tiring day. Before we left we wished our companions all the best and hoped they wouldn't have too bad a time with leeches. They cast disparaging glances at our footwear and remarked that we ought not to get bitten. We all wore boots and puttees.

The nine miles up the 4,000 ft to Penlong La seem long, but the conditions were much better than coming down. No leeches and little water to wade through. The big landslide was much the same, still a track over the loose sand of the slide. B & I tried to climb up the landslide and slithered about hanging on to the loose earth like flies on a wall. However, like Bruce's spider, we eventually made sufficient progress to catch on to something more solid. Stanley was just above us and Jessie made a still different detour with Ila, the pair of them disappearing for nearly an hour. They joined the path further on having had a bad time wading round in mud.

We had our lunch on the Penlong La looking towards Gantok. It was a fine view. The last bit of the road was pleasant but we were glad to reach the bungalow and find it empty and a welcome awaiting us from the old, toothless Chaukidar. The bungalow was very palatial, having two large bedrooms and a pleasant sitting room with a fire. We had the most incredible gala dinner with many courses, ending with peaches and egg custard.

What was left of the stores we gave to the boys. They were to continue on foot and we by bus.

KALIMPONG – 4,100 ft
Monday, 24 July 1944

I woke early to find the whole range of mountains visible – a really wonderful sight. They seemed far off, but it was easy to identify the peaks from a chart hanging on the wall. In the sunrise once again the snows appeared as pure gold, only this time there were no clouds and we could see the intervening foothills folding into the distance.

Dawa Tundup and Gylgen produced their Himalayan books for us to write a chit. We did so gladly and found many fine tributes from famous climbers of all nationalities, including Ruttledge. They had both been on two Everest expeditions and on Kanchenjunga (twice) and K2, and Dawa Tundup had been on Nanga Parbat. His chit on this occasion was written by the British Liaison Officer, and he said Dawa Tundup was the only high climber porter to survive the avalanche. After this he volunteered for every attempted rescue and was outstanding in his behaviour. He had a large certificate signed by Hitler, Paul Bauer and a Red Cross person. It was the German Red Cross Certificate for bravery.

These two were Himalayan porters. These are known as the Tigers and after being on a Himalayan Expedition are enrolled and given a book for chits.

They have a small badge with a tiger's head and inscription and their number on the back.

We were sad to see them go and they all said farewells and were off. We watched them disappear down the road and then waited for our bus. Eventually we were piled in with our bedding rolls and had a rather miserable journey down to Tista Bridge. It was very hot and we consoled ourselves that the two cars would soon arrive.

The road down was in good condition, though landslides are frequent, closing the road for days at a time. The Tista Bridge is modern and well constructed. The river at that point is wide and swift.

Bernard went to the local police station and on contacting Mr Kydd by phone he discovered that the cars had never been sent off – somehow, in spite of two letters giving the exact time and date, he was expecting us two days later. Tempers were a bit frayed as he suggested we camped by the roadside, having no food or protection from the numerous mosquitoes, only bedding. After many efforts we managed to find a big car, but this could not negotiate the narrow road to

Darjeeling. Only Austin 7s and the like could pass. This meant going to Kalimpong, a distance of nine-and-a-half miles, and staying the night. We have managed to put up at this one, the Himalayan by name, but not so good.

There was a fine view tonight from the veranda, looking over all the foothills, but the snows were hidden in mist.

This is our first taste of civilisation after three weeks in the wide open spaces. It is an unpleasant jar and I feel very unsociable and hostile to all around me in the hotel. The dirty or rather pitying looks they cast at well worn travellers with dirty hobnailed boots and shorts ... I am reminded of Peter Fleming's remarks when he and his partner arrived in Srinagar after six months in the wilds. For complete lack of enthusiasm in anything of real interest the average European out here takes a lot of beating.

We had an early dinner, but thought Gylgen's cooking far better. We got a few scandalised looks at the huge appetites we had. We felt like going through the menu twice.

DARJEELING
Tuesday, 25 July 1944

We left early by the same big car for Darjeeling. Having to go by the big road it entailed a distance of 42 miles down to Siliguri in the plains at sea level, and then up the tortuous road to Darjeeling, another 54 miles. The journey was hot and unpleasant and

11

Hospital Ship *Melchior Treub*

As has been related earlier, when war started I was in South Africa with my sister Mary. I returned home in January 1940. I joined the Army Q.A.I.M.N.S.(R.) and after a year at Aldershot I was posted to Ninth Casualty Clearing Station (C.C.S.). We assembled in Knightshays Court, Tiverton and sailed for India in March 1942. We helped in several hospitals where there was a great shortage of trained nursing staff. We ended up in Chittagong, which was very hard work. Word came for the Unit to move to the forward area. The Matron for India, Miss Wilkinson, visited us and said the forward area would be too near the Japanese, and the Sisters would be a liability as several had been captured and some killed in the earlier part of the war, therefore there was no point in us being in the Unit and we must be replaced by men. The Sisters were all posted to other Units, and I was offered a hospital ship and was posted to the S.S. *Melchior Treub* – Hospital Ship No. 6.

I had sailed on the S.S. *Melchior Treub* when I was sent on a theatre course, and when I was disembarking comments were made about the quantity of baggage for someone serving with a C.C.S. unit (the allowance being one bedding-roll, kitbag, trunk and haversack). I had added a small tin trunk and a bicycle. On my posting to S.S. *Melchior Treub* I travelled by train and then by boat all night, followed by another train to Calcutta. I went to the women's service hostel where I was made very welcome. I asked the warden if I could leave some of my belongings to be collected later, and my request was granted. So at last I set off for my hospital ship. I arrived at the riverbank and hailed a sampan.

I was received on board by an officer who introduced himself as Chief Officer Soep. "Welcome aboard, Sister Roger!" He took me to meet the Matron and then showed me where I would be working. This was the surgical ward, which included the theatre. This had been the promenade deck – now converted into a ward of 100 cots, two of which were large single cots, the remainder being doubles. The Chief Officer handed me the keys, saying, "If there is anything that I can do, please do not hesitate to ask." Subsequently he said, "I did not know whom I was giving that information to – they were not requests but urgent demands!"

Later when I went to look at the theatre I was horrified to see the plain shelves and cupboards, and a post mortem table screwed into the middle of the deck. What was the use of such a theatre if we had an emergency in bad weather? My needs were considerable and rather urgent.

I met Captain Stanley Chapman, the surgeon. He was older than I and was an orthopaedic surgeon in

Worthing. We looked at the equipment and our accommodation and decided that we needed changes and more equipment – but how? The next day, walking along in Calcutta, I met an officer with whom I had worked when training in midwifery. We caught up with the news and he told me that he was with a special mobile unit with every kind of equipment. I told my news and of the problems I had, and he told me to go to an army store and that they would give us all that we needed. Thanking him most sincerely, I returned to the ship to see Stanley and we made a list of our needs. We then went to see Colonel Carr, our C.O. He gladly gave his permission to order the necessary supplies. Next day Stanley and I (who were now using Christian names) set off sandwiched into a rickshaw, with much laughter from the Colonel! At the army store we were welcomed and told to go round and choose what we wanted. We forgot our list and chose all that we needed, including a superb operating table. With very many thanks we returned to our ship absolutely delighted, and the goods were delivered immediately. When the army authorities discovered what had happened they made sure that no one else would have the same good luck. Stanley told Colonel Carr that he thought that I imagined I was in Woolworths.

Next day we set to and arranged all our new equipment, and then we contacted the Chief Officer (now known as Bernard) and asked him for his help. Out went the post mortem table and the new one was screwed into the deck. The trolley had wooden blocks fitted over the wheels, and everything was put in its place on the shelves and cupboards. The Ship's Carpenter worked hard and made a magnificent job.

Our theatre was now stormproof. Stanley and I gave Bernard a big thank you.

At this point I must tell you a little bit of the Colonel's story which Bernard omitted.

When war broke out Colonel Carr, who as a T.A. Officer had previously been called up and was already in charge of a small British military hospital in Penang, found himself and his charges were getting closer to the front line by the day, and realised that they would have to move out fast. The authorities left him to his own resources and advised him to do as he thought necessary. So joining up with an army Major who had escaped from the Japanese they were fortunate enough to get in touch with a Captain Wu, the C.O. and owner of a small hospital ship the S.S. *Wusueh*, and filled it with staff, patients and others. They sailed the 1,200 miles to Ceylon (see *The Miracle*, chapter 8 above) and eventually ended up in Calcutta, India.

When the monsoon weather started the S.S.*Wusueh* was not suitable for that type of weather, being shallow draught, so the staff were transferred to three different troopships which were taking troops to Chittagong and bringing walking patients back to Calcutta; but this was not in agreement with the Geneva Convention. Due to Colonel Carr's vigorous efforts, S.S. *Melchior Treub* was chosen instead of either of the two B.I. (British India Steam Navigation Company) ships, to be converted to Hospital Ship No. 6.

One more thing I had to do was to make up packs of dressings and sterilise them. I was used to an autoclave, but this one was full of holes. The Chief Engineer was watching the proceedings and I was told that this was no job for a lady. I replied that I was a nurse and was experienced with this machine.

Now down to the Colonel: "Oh, dear, that means a letter to Delhi and at least six months before we have it back." I told him that I knew the manager of Garden Reach workshops and I was sure that he would help. "On your bike then, girl." I enjoyed my run and had a warm welcome and was promised an immediate repair. On my return a thunderstorm with pouring rain broke out. I was soaked but welcomed back with relief, safe and sound. My autoclave was hoisted into place in two days, my dressing packs were sterilised and now I could reorganise the work.

My staff consisted of a British sergeant, three British other ranks and half a dozen Indians including a lance nike – a lance corporal. Stanley was the surgeon. On the deck below the medical ward and in a converted hold for walking patients, the Sister in here was also the relief.

On our first trip we found the problem of the caste system. They could only do approved tasks. Then I discovered a wonderful word – 'dispensation' – for the duration of the war. I explained that we were all nurses and that we all looked after our patients' needs, including bedpans and serving food. After disembarking all had to be thoroughly cleaned and made ready for the next patients. Our ward had been the promenade deck and had to be cleaned with sea water and sand and then 'holy stoned'. This was done by sailors, but the decks below floors were linoleum and had to be washed by ward staff. This was felt to be rather unfair, so I asked our Chief Officer for his help, and a team of sailors taught my boys, who, with great enthusiasm and with bare feet, were taught a sailor's job and were very proud.

At this point I must describe the layout of the ship. The main deck aft was the area for the kitchens for patients and the Indian other ranks. This included a space for a goat to be used for their food. I was an animal lover and made sure that the goat had the best possible care, with plenty of water and food. I use to talk to it and rub its ears. (More of this later!) The medical ward was situated forward on this deck. The remaining first class cabins were for medical and female nursing staff. The nursing staff were on port side, and the medical on starboard, with the Colonel in between.

I had my bike aboard, and Colonel Carr suggested that it should be kept outside his cabin. This suited me, but caused the Colonel some embarrassment later when a senior officer visited and told him that when he was inspecting a hospital ship, a Sister had a bicycle. Mine was clearly visible on the way to my cabin – so I could not take him there.

Our cabins were very comfortable, a bunk under the porthole, a settee and space for a small trunk. Mine contained a portable gramophone and records. The door had to be left open in case of ship's damage, so I had a curtain instead. Matron's cabin was bigger, as it was also her office. There were three Sisters. I had the surgical department, another the medical and a third (who was also relief) the walking cases.

The bathing arrangements were unusual. Standing on a slatted board was a large tank of fresh water from which you baled water over yourself, and, after soaping, baled more water. This was a good way of saving water. Once someone jumped into the tank of water, causing big problems!

We were well looked after by a Javanese boy called Doul. He was older than the others but he was very attentive, bringing early morning tea etc. He decided that his duties included care of my bicycle. Bernard was amazed to find him busy with it when he was off duty. The officers had a boy each. Bernard's was Karan and once, when I was doing a spell of night duty and on my last round, I was followed by Karan with a tray and a large glass of lime and water with a liberal helping of glucose. Karan would not return to his boss until I sat down in my office and finished the drink. Bernard thought that this drink was just what I needed!

There was a balcony outside our cabins and, on the deck below, a lounge, with comfortable chairs and a piano. Stanley was a very good pianist. We shared facilities with the ship's officers, including a fine dining saloon, very good food and no wartime rations. On Sundays we had ricestaffel. This consisted of fried egg, various meats and vegetables with spice flavours. The officers had theirs on soup plates. The catering was done by Goanese. Another language that the ship's officers had to speak (as well as English) was Hindustani, and Malay for Javanese. How poor we are at languages. In the evenings some played bridge, but that was not for me. I enjoyed sitting in my cabin and playing my records. Stanley sometimes joined me and looked after the records. After a time, there would be a knock at the door and Bernard would appear, pipe in hand. He would join us and we would spend a pleasant evening. As time went on this became almost a routine when at sea and I made us a concoction of chocolate and Horlicks, which we enjoyed whilst chatting.

One time when I was sitting in my cabin I had an unusual visitor – my friend the goat! Having rubbed his head he must have got my scent. Happily, he let me lead him back to his quarters, walking through the medical ward, much to the amusement of the patients.

We had several quiet trips, and we were notified of numbers of British and Indians troops or prisoners, allowing us to order suitable food.

I had another bout of amoebic dysentery and was in hospital when a Sister was admitted with the same complaint and occupied the next bed to me. We knew each other and had already met in the swimming pool. We were both sent on sick leave at the same time and went to Ninital, a place in the hilly area. After an all-day train journey, we had an amusing incident when we had to change trains in Lucknow, when we were going into the town for a meal. I was stopped by the Army police, as I was improperly dressed, being without a hat. I was in khaki and had forgotten my rather smart khaki beret. However, he was a kindly person and thought that if we went quickly perhaps we would manage.

We enjoyed ourselves, then I thought that as I was so near to the Himalayas I should go up to Ranikhet. I was invited to stay in the Sister's Mess. It was a marvellous place with a small hospital. Next morning I set off with some sandwiches and a pony up on to the ridge. Oh, what a view – beyond the valley the whole horizon of Himalayan snow-covered giants; the nearest was Nanda Devi at 25,643 feet. A German expedition had a disastrous accident there with many casualties and some deaths. One of our Sherpas with us later had been awarded the German Red Cross for his bravery in rescues.

I was in my element and cantered along singing away to my horse, just so happy and grateful to have such a privilege. Eventually I found a good spot, tethered my steed and had lunch and then wrote a letter home. What a wonderful little expedition, and all in the middle of the war. So the next day back to my friend in Ninital and back to work, much refreshed.

As the battle for Kohima became fiercer, the casualties increased and we carried a greater number of patients, including some Japanese prisoners. On another trip I had half the ward with prisoners, and they were the dregs of the army. They lay in their cots looking rather frightened. The weather was very rough. And we had seen to all our own men, and the smells were bad. Stanley said he had had enough and departed. My corporal and my faithful lance nike took the trolley and I did the dressings, leaving each one clean and comfortable and with such a look of gratitude. They had been told that they would be tortured and killed. I hope they told a different story if they got home.

Working in those bad weather conditions proved once again that if there is a job to be dealt with there is no room for seasickness or even fear.

The battle for Kohima was increasing and the casualties were much heavier. The serious ones were flown out to specialist hospitals, but on this occasion when we had over a hundred stretcher cases and had disembarked them in Calcutta, most of them were re-embarked and we were ordered to sail for Madras. We were pleased to have more time with our patients. On our return to Chittagong we took on more casualties, some of whom were very badly wounded men that needed more nursing. One lad had a very badly infected leg and he had lost a lot of blood; his condition was poor and he needed a blood transfusion. Many were the offers, but the Chief Officer was of the right blood group and so was chosen. We kept special watch on our lad. He was so brave, and I had a chat with him later when I was sitting beside him. His name was Hillcott and he lived in Paisley; he was pleased to know that my home was fairly near, in Gourock. He told me that his wife was expecting their first baby and he did not want her to be worried. He was in one of the special single cots, which was much easier for nursing.

Next day I looked at his wound and saw that he had developed gas gangrene. I felt the awful feeling of the crackling of the gas in the wound. Now that we used M and B antibiotic, this was unheard of. Stanley came at once and explained to our lad that he would have to operate right away and remove his leg to save his life. He was so good and gave his permission.

The weather had deteriorated, and the ship was rolling and pitching. Stanley sent a message to the bridge asking for the ship to be steadied for twenty minutes as we had an operation to perform. The ship hove to, and Stanley did a fine job and at speed. The team worked very well, and all the storm proofing was a great success. A big thanks to the ship's carpenter – our only breakage was one glass syringe. Our patient was still poorly and needed plasma. This was stored and only needed sterile water to be added and then given intravenously, and by evening our lad was very much better. When we docked at Madras the other casualties were put on a hospital train to take them to a holding hospital. According to Stanley, when Hillcott was being carried over the ramp, a stretcher-bearer stumbled and our lad swore in fluent Dutch. He was going to a local Indian hospital next day.

The docks were some distance from the town, and next day Bernard and I set off on our bikes (Bernard having acquired one). We had a very warm welcome from Hillcott; few of the staff spoke English. I asked him if he would like me to write to his wife, and my mother to send some baby clothes. He was delighted and we left him with all good wishes.

Once more back at Chittagong, we loaded over one hundred casualties. The weather was atrocious, with very rough seas and pouring rain. This time the ship was damaged. The Captain contacted headquarters and said that he would proceed to Calcutta. Later he was congratulated for a wise decision. The patients were disembarked and the ship was to go into dry dock for at least five weeks. The Captain and Colonel Carr decided this was a chance to catch up on leave. That was how Matron, Stanley, Bernard and I set off for Darjeeling and the Sebu La, a pass of 3,700 feet. (That is another story, which you have just read.)

12

Marion, Our Sister Sahib

When we returned a month later the war had moved on. Penicillin was now in use for patients at risk. The patients on the drug had a large label attached to them, and we were given supplies from the forward areas. The doses were every four hours and were supplied in individual files. Each dose had to be mixed with sterile water – rather a performance. The Indian rules for drugs were different from ours. They were only interested in those sold on the black market – M.B. and mepacrine – a tablet form of quinine of which all the troops had to take one each day. Stanley and I kept strict control of our dangerous drugs, but had a very simple way with the others. We counted the tablets at the beginning of the trip and at the end subtracted the number of patients, so giving a satisfactory result.

It was a sad day when our very special Colonel Carr was posted. He was perfect for the job. He had no time for red tape: all that mattered was the best for the patients. After the war we told him of our marriage and he was delighted. We kept in touch with him and, after he died, with his wife and later his daughter.

The Burma coast must be one of the least attractive on earth. No rivers, little habitation, perhaps some fishermen, but south of Chittagong till the Burmese border, just one human habitation – Cox's Bazaar – and then nothing until Akyab (Sitwe), hundreds of miles southwards. When we returned from our trek in the Himalayas to the ship, it was several weeks before we were ready to take up our duties.

The war was moving on and the advance down the Arakan road became steady, and very slowly our troops pushed the Japanese southwards. In October we had orders to proceed down the coast and to anchor four miles off the coast to be within reach of Cox's Bazaar.

There was nothing to take a bearing on, just to make a rough guess. One could vaguely see a mountain range, which was ten miles from the coast and ran parallel to it with one highway in between from Cox's Bazaar to Akyab.

We anchored as near as possible to the C.C.S. and the coast. This was twenty miles north of the battle zone. This time we had to embark our casualties from the C.C.S. to the ship, twelve miles over rough terrain. There were no jetties, so this was accomplished by using an amphibious vehicle or 'dukw'. It took the dukw two hours, which was a long time and exhausting for the patients. When the dukw reached the sea a lever turned it into an amphibious vehicle, so bringing our casualties to the ship.

Now we had to embark our casualties with the aid of cargo gear. Our Chief Officer took all the necessary precautions. A gentle swell of two to three feet kept the ship on an easy roll, and it would require muscle power to prevent the derricks from swinging. Stretchers were placed on a pallet and were hoisted one at a time, with a sailor standing by to forestall sliding. The Chief Officer kept his crew busy with checking everything. The heavy pallets (5ft x 5ft), new slings with four arms and sewn in hooks, new guy ropes etc, etc. Nothing could be left to chance, when loading such precious human cargo. These instructions were given by the Chief Officer.

This was a slow operation, and when we had them safely on the deck they were soon in a comfortable cot and given ice cold drinks. These embarkations were lengthy, but we did not depend on the tide. It took two days to embark 210 casualties, and then back to Chittagong and finally our casualties were disembarked.

Later we had very urgent orders to proceed at once to pick up casualties at Foul River. We were not even given time to fill to capacity with fuel and fresh water. This was the moment that we had been waiting for. An abundance of dressing packs were sterilised, the emergency boxes of intravenous fluids were checked. Our destination was well down the coast. It was lovely weather and I just sat on our little bit of deck and thoroughly enjoyed myself watching the scenery and dreaming of Scotland.

When we arrived at the mouth of the river the Captain said that he would not take his ship up, as he had not been there before. However, the Chief Officer was happy to take over as he had been there before. Up anchor, and away we sailed, slithering over a sandbank.

There were sounds of gunfire and tank landing craft – the latter called L.C.T.s – sailing to and fro. A launch approached us and a senior officer asked us if he could help. We told him that we had been sent urgently to pick up casualties. He told us that they were advancing and that there were no casualties. We waited till next day when a conference was held and it was decided that the surgeon and the Chief Officer should go ashore and try to make their way to Akyab. They managed to get a lift and, sure enough, the casualties were there. Eventually they got back to us and we sailed with as much speed as possible down the coast to Akyab. A large number of badly wounded British casualties were embarked, strapped on their stretchers. They had been previously treated in a casualty clearing station. We made them as comfortable as possible and gave them something to eat.

We were anchored out in the bay and suddenly the alarm bells rang. All our training came into immediate action – haversacks, tin hats on, to our wards – and the ship's lifeboats were slung out. Planes circling overhead were Japanese. If we were attacked and had to take to the boats, the stretchers had to be lowered into the sea, feet first, with the earnest hope that they would float. I will never forget the wonderful bravery of those men, with a grin, just accepting the situation. I felt proud to be British. This was no time to be frightened – there was work to be done. More aircraft, but this time they were ours and the sky was theirs. What a cheer went up from all! But where were my Indians? They had scrambled into the lifeboats – what a blasting they had from their Indian officers with threats of much punishment, but that was not necessary. My boys were very ashamed and I explained that in future they should just come to the ward and Chief Officer would tell us what to do.

After all the drama we set off for Calcutta, picking up more patients from Chittagong and on the way happily handing over our patients. After a big clean up, we refilled with stores and on this occasion, of course, with oil and fresh water – then we were off again down the coast, this time to Ramree Island, situated just south of Akyab.

When we arrived, an L.C.T. came alongside. We were hanging over the rails watching with interest when an officer called out, "Hello, Marion, what are you doing?" This was an R.A.M.C. Major who had sailed to India with us in 1942. He told us that he had patients for us though we had to wait, but he invited me to come and see what they were doing. After a little discussion Bernard and I went ashore with him and had a fascinating time. They had taken over the island without any opposition. The Japanese troops were big men from north Japan.

We were shown over the L.C.T. The door could be lowered on to the beach and casualties could be treated on the spot and taken aboard where everything was available. There was a generator to supply electricity. There was a fridge, so that they were able to use intravenous infusions and give urgent surgical treatment. This would make the most wonderful difference to the comfort and recovery. After our troops had been treated it was the turn of the prisoners. This had an immediate effect, as they realised that the stories they had been told of the torture and mutilation and probable death were untrue. As a result they gave all the information they had, and this proved to be accurate. They had also been given special titbits such as tinned fruit.

Cheduba was an island nearby, whose civilians had been evacuated for some reason, and we were to accommodate them for a time. This was somewhat unusual, and no one seemed to find a language that they could understand, but one really old lady managed to convey an urgent need for a cigar, and this was granted. Next day, the cruiser H.M.S. *Newcastle* arrived and relieved us of our unexpected visitors, and we had to prepare for the seriously injured Japanese who had given such valuable information. They were to be nursed in the two special beds. More of our own casualties were taken aboard, and during the trip we made our way back to Calcutta, picking up further casualties on the way.

In between times we had some happy events with the ship's officers. We planned a Christmas party, and our Irish Sister met some members of E.N.S.A. and asked them if they would come and entertain us at our party. They were to catch a plane for the forward area to entertain the troops that were in need of a change. We assured them that they would be put ashore in good time, so they agreed.

We had a wonderful time, starting with the Christmas tree and presents for all. I had a very beautiful picture from the Captain and a big hug as well! I tried to get them all to dance 'Strip the Willow', but without success. A very fine buffet followed, including Christmas cake and as much to drink as we wanted. Gin was the choice of the officers, except for Bernard, so (apart from a glass of wine), we stuck to ginger ale. Likewise our entertainers, who played their instruments (whilst we all joined in the singing with great gusto), well into the early hours. Bernard and I watched the time and took our friends ashore. With very grateful thanks and big hugs they were away.

The following year, 1944, we had another Christmas at sea, carrying only Indian patients. Matron, Bernard and I decided that we would give them a Christmas party. We made up parcels and dressed Bernard as Santa, complete with white beard and red cloak. A real party, and the Indian officers said we were daft as the men would not understand, but they greatly enjoyed themselves.

When we were in Calcutta we were anchored close to the shore and we could have a wander along the Median, which was a park area. There were seats, but the military police did not allow us to sit down!!

One evening, Bernard said that he must get back on board, as the Bore was due. When spring tides were due, at every high tide a large wave called a Bore made its way up the river and all ships had to be ready.

We were anchored some distance from the shore with another ship further out. For good measure we were anchored fore and aft with two anchors with enormous chains and these would hold the ship.

As the Bore started coming up the river a cry could be heard – "Bore aagai (coming)!" and little crafts could be seen tossing about. The officers and crew were standing by ready for any trouble. The wave hit us, but our anchors held, and it passed up the Hooglie with less strength!

If we were ashore, we could visit shops and a very fine café and bakery with lovely cream cakes. Also in the afternoons, sometimes, there was a tea dance, and Bernard was a very good dancer. I was fairly good, but was defeated by the tango. I was told that to dance it properly the partners should be in love (but I only had to pretend). In the evenings the two big hotels had dinner dances, and that was very enjoyable.

If we were in port on a Sunday we tried to go to a church where there was a very popular minister. So many members of the Services attended that extra seats had to be found. People started arriving so early that records were played until the service began. All were made so welcome and afterwards refreshments were served in the hall. Some of the British women were not too ready to invite the ordinary Tommies into their drawing rooms – these men, who were the salt of the earth and who had been fighting in appalling conditions. This minister spoke out on this subject very strongly. Bernard and I always remembered the special hymns that we all sang in that church, for example, "I need Thee, oh, I need Thee," and Scottish Psalms.

Unfortunately, soon afterwards I went down with a *fourth* dose of amoebic dysentery – probably as a result of only being treated with Epsom salts with my first attack. This latest was my second attack since being on the ship. The Officers hospital was in what had been the Japanese Embassy. I was really fed up, as I knew that the course of treatment would be four weeks. Unfortunately a girl just out with ENSA was in the next bed with dysentery and then was diagnosed with cholera, and I developed it. I had not had my inoculation, as I was not well. The result was rather dramatic, being found in a heap in some odd corner. Poor Bernard was somewhat alarmed when visiting the next day. The M.O. told him that I would be sent home as soon as I was able to travel and said that I must never return to the tropics.

Bernard returned to the ship and wrote to head office giving his resignation and asking for it to take effect from the end of the war.

Needless to say, I made a rapid recovery and the Medical Board decided to downgrade me, which meant taking me off the ship, thereafter returning to Britain in due course. I was very sorry to leave my special *'Treub'* but it was the right decision. Matron Jessie came up to see me, was very kind and was glad that I was able to take leave and that we would have a special holiday.

We were quite a cheery crowd in the ward. The ship sailed to Cochin in southwest India, but Bernard got his leave and came to Calcutta, and we set off by train to Ootacamund in the area of the Niligris. It was a journey of several days, and there was a box filled with ice to keep us cool. Refreshments were provided at intervals, and once a day we were asked if we would like to have dinner at the next suitable station.

The train stopped and the meal that had been ordered some hours before was served, and when the diners were ready the train moved on.

Once when travelling alone I was the only diner, and yet the same arrangements were available. It was fascinating seeing the different country at a leisurely pace and watching the inhabitants going about their work. Since writing this story the names of some of these towns or places have been changed.

We arrived in Ootacamund and had to find somewhere to sleep. We were directed to the Club and Bernard was given a bed, but there was nowhere for me except the ladies' cloakroom, for three nights.

After much wandering about we visited a lady who said firmly: "No." (We must have looked like a couple of strays – I was only about six stones). "You will both come and stay in our home." Celia Broadhurst's husband was a tea planter; the plantation was some distance away. They had two boys, but because of the war they could not go to Britain for their schooling.

We thoroughly enjoyed our holiday away from all service life. When our leave was up, Bernard went to Bombay and I was posted to a military hospital with a families section. I was on night duty for the hospital when the news came that the War was over. I was busy delivering a baby, but a little later I went over to the men and told them and we had a little celebration.

We did not know about the atomic bomb, but later we heard that the Indians, Chinese and Burmese were working together so well that the officers felt that given a little longer they might have helped to achieve victory without the bomb and that good relationships with the Burmese would have remained. This was written in one of his mountaineering books by Lt. Colonel Spencer Chapman of the Regular army, who was the officer in charge of the Jungle Warfare Unit.

A little later I received orders to join a group of Sisters to go to Bombay and join a troopship. I sent Bernard a telegram saying, "Arriving 3pm departing 6pm meet you at the bank". I asked permission from the Sister-in-charge of our group if I could go to the bank, but as the train drew in an officer in naval uniform was meeting us. No; I did not need to go to the bank; the bank had come to me!

Bernard took charge and escorted us to the troop ship S.S. S*icilia.* We were welcomed by the Chief Officer, McVicar, who presumed that Bernard was effectively in charge. We were in Bombay for some days, and the Sisters took it in turns to be on duty. My day was on Bernard's birthday, and the steward made a fine cake complete with candle and name. We sailed, but knew that we were both going to Singapore. S.S. *Melchior Treub* was there first, and as we sailed into the bay Bernard, as usual, was alongside to give a welcome.

As we were in Singapore for nearly two weeks, on my days off Bernard took me to visit some of his fellow officers who were still in Changi Jail until arrangements could be made for their medical treatment and ships to take them to their homes, depending on the state of the Islands.

We went into the jail, and it was an awful experience: the men were skin and bone. Bernard was greeted by name, but he could not recognise any of them. We talked, and they were so pleased to see a white woman. We did some shopping and bought things that had been buried to hide them from the Japanese.

When I was in a shop I met a Barts Nurse, Margo Turner, who was in the Q.A.I.M.N.S. and had been evacuated, torpedoed, hanging on to a raft for days and picked up by a Japanese naval ship. The ship's doctor was so impressed that he kept her until he felt she was fit enough to be transferred to a prison camp. Later she became Matron-in-chief.

Margo Turner was decorated by the Queen and became Dame Margo Turner, having been promoted to Brigadier Q.A.I.M.N.S. and later President of the League of St Bartholemew's Nurses on her retirement. Sadly, she died in St Dunstain's Hospital as a result of her wartime experiences

The big day came when Admiral Mountbatten took the surrender with much ceremony, a wonderful experience. Now it was time for us to go our separate ways, but first I went to my very special ship and saw those that I still knew. Then, a wonderful surprise. My Indian Boys came running round me with hands clasped and all excited, crying, "Our Sister Sahib." What a welcome! That was the most wonderful compliment that I have ever had and remains a very special memory. We were a happy team – all different religions, castes and sects working together to look after our patients. Now the country is divided and they are all fighting each other.

Bernard saw me to my ship the S.S. *Sicilia,* turning without looking back to the ship. We were both dreaming of our future.

13

Home from the War and off to Venezuela

I left Singapore on the troopship S.S. *Sicilia*, carrying ex-prisoners of war just recently rescued. We had been warned by the Red Cross that the women might be a little difficult as, when they were rescued and arrived in Singapore expecting a special welcome, hundreds were already being cared for, so only basic needs could be dealt with. Washing facilities, food and clothing were available, but the only garments were khaki shirts and slacks, which most of them refused, instead coming aboard in brief shorts and bikini tops.

On board the men were on troop decks similar to the accommodation they had on the way out. The women were in large cabins and had their meals in the first class dining saloon, much to the consternation of the ship's officers.

The first call was Ceylon, where the Red Cross came aboard and provided toilet necessities. Then on to Suez, where it was cooler but still no khaki. Arrangements were made, however, for all to go ashore, where there were large marquees marked for the different services and a big one for the women, who were provided with all manner of garments and a suitcase. The women emerged as ladies.

Another Sister and I had the women's ward and we nursed a really wonderful little lady. She had been an orthopaedic surgeon in the hospital in Singapore and had Chinese students. She had spent the whole war in Changi Jail. She was so content and grateful for all the help that she had from her students, who managed to smuggle toiletries and what they considered essentials in to her, e.g. sanitary towels. There was a big bag of wool and she spent her time sorting and rolling up balls.

Eventually we reached home and docked at Liverpool, where I had a message to wait for my brother George, who was a navigator with Shackletons in the R.A.F. Thereafter we headed home to Gourock. It was near to Christmas, and what a wonderful celebration we had. After a short spell in an army hospital, in February 1946 I was demobbed.

Bernard was eventually free to come to Gourock; he was on his way by a cargo ship so the wedding was planned. My sister Mary and family were on leave from South Africa and the house was full. My father decided that we should be married in Brodick on the Isle of Arran, as the family would be there on holiday. He said that May was unlucky, so it could be on 30 April 1946. Our very dear Minister of Ashton Church, Rev. George McNab, was delighted and said that he would take the ceremony.

Bernard's ship was very slow. At last, however, he landed at Liverpool, and I was there to meet him. He leapt off the ship but was asked by the Immigration Officer for his visa. Bernard did not know about such a thing. He was told that he had 90 hours to leave the country. He explained that he was getting married in six days' time in Scotland.

The officer was really marvellous and just said, "Off to Scotland and tell them your story." So we did, and he allowed us to carry on and after our honeymoon to go to London and sort things.

My brother George met us, and a lawyer had to arrange a marriage contract at my father's instructions. The lawyer was horrified, "The wedding must be postponed; after all you might have to live in Holland." He was overruled but told my brother that his young sister was very stubborn and hoped that she would not live to rue it.

The wedding was such a happy occasion, in lovely spring weather, and in a little country church. Finally we managed to get off the island on the steamer S.S. *Glen Sannox* for our honeymoon.

We returned to a flat in Gourock.

After visiting Bernard's brother Leo and family in France we then settled down. Bernard went job hunting, but despite his considerable qualifications, particularly in languages, he had no success and he did not want to go back to sea. As we had hoped, a baby was expected, and John arrived with a head of red hair. We moved in with my parents after my sister Mary and the children had returned to South Africa. The little grandson was a great joy to them.

Eventually we decided that we would run a hotel, and we looked at many. I was going to do the cooking and Bernard was to look after the guests. We found the ideal place in Skelmorlie; fortunately there was a phone call for Bernard to go to London for an interview with the Marine Superintendent of the Shell Oil Company – and so to Venezuela in a river tug.

14

The Chart

By Captain Bernard Soep

This first appeared as an article in the Nautical Magazine, *Vol. 232, No. 6, December 1984, and is reprinted here, by courtesy of the Editor.*

Hardly a month goes by, nowadays, that we are not told of some intrepid soul, male or female, alone or in company, crossing the North Atlantic, or somebody else just finished circumnavigating the world. They don't lack enterprise or courage, use simple navigation methods in the old style: a sextant and their own calculations, or the aid of the latest nautical equipment: satellite navigation and computers – the push button method. They have one thing in common: they all need charts. "Of course," one would say. There is no "of course" about it. The other day I read of somebody who had sailed to the other side of the Atlantic with the sole aid of a school atlas; I don't know how this was achieved, but I would rather have some reliable charts to make a correct landfall after some 3,000 miles.

Still, I was faced with just the same situation: no charts, not even a pilot chart, on which, though not precise, one can chart and plan a course.

I had just signed on with a big oil company to take a tug from Rotterdam to Maracaibo as Chief Officer. A grandiose name in this case, as the only other officer was a young man fresh from nautical college who had his Second Mate's ticket. Though I could not know it, I was in for a number of surprises. The first came in a meeting with my Captain; he was walking on the quayside when I arrived with my gear. "Are you Mr. Soep?" I said that I was. He looked like the shopkeeper from round the corner, no jacket, in his short sleeves, his trousers held up by his red braces over his very well developed tummy. Very friendly, he was smoking a huge Meerschaum pipe, showing a trail of tobacco juice down his shirt; the result was that he produced an enormous red handkerchief to wipe the spittle away, making it even worse. He had a red, round face, which made him look less like a sailor than anything else.

"Did you bring a sextant?" When I said yes, I had, he continued, "You have to do all the navigation; I have not used an instrument since 1930. I was 15 years in the West Indies with the same company and never needed one; I know those waters like the fingers on my hand."

He had been retired since just before the War and survived the German occupation, hence his eagerness to have this job; it paid very well.

It was one of those summers when it never stops blowing and raining. To add to the misery, sailing was delayed again and again, not by the weather (nobody gave that a thought); no, by defects in the engine room. The man in charge, the Chief Engineer, was a very able and competent man, as time would prove, but he had to deal with an engine entirely new to him: a diesel electric. All the auxiliaries were electric; even the steering had fingertip control, he said.

We had three trial runs in pouring rain, all showing defects, but at last the Chief was satisfied.

The tug had been built by Todd in New Jersey during the War for salvage purposes. A number of these had been built towards the end of the War to help in clearing the harbours of Europe.

Of approximately 480 tons, length 70 feet, width 21 ft and draught 11 ft, sturdy and seaworthy, she resembled a flatiron more than anything else and behaved like one, riding the sea at a maximum speed of 12 knots. We carried an extra 40 drums of fuel, 42 gallons each, on the towing deck, which had the Chief's and my own special care, by having them properly secured; no towing cables were carried on this trip. She was of course all engine room, with the accommodation built above and around it, six cabins in all and two store rooms. On S.B. side fore with entrance to (a) engine room (b) two greasers, (c) the Second Mate and the motor driver, (d) mess room and galley. On port side from aft (a) the cabin for the Chief and myself, (b) next, the Cook/steward and one A.B., (c) last, cabin for two A.B.s and, to finish the other side of the galley cum mess room, another locker. On top of this was the bridge and Captain's quarters including chart table, and above this again a small monkey deck with reserve compass. No radio but a radiotelephone with a range of only 200 miles. I brought my own radio to listen to the weather forecasts, an excellent Philips which I was able to use for almost the whole trip. Our toilet, the one and only one, was in the top corner of the engine room, nice and cosy.

Total complement: eleven, including the Captain. This bridge is completely closed in, 7 ft by 4 ft, chart table behind the steersman, the Captain's bunk behind that, some lockers and a washbasin; notwithstanding the continuous deluge of water, real dry and comfortable. There was some comfort for the Captain: sliding door between his bunk and the rest.

At last we sailed with the Venezuelan flag of yellow, blue and red flying lustily from the only masthead, meaning that we were under Venezuelan nationality. It was raining cats and dogs, a short choppy sea, windforce 7/8 and we were immediately under water more than on it. Communication between the cabins and the bridge was a rather acrobatic feat, accomplished by clambering over the two foot high coaming, stepping gingerly over the gangway backwards by holding onto the handrail six inches above the bridge deck, I think just for this purpose, and feet in Wellingtons on the lower rating, side stepping till opposite the vertical steel ladder, which led into the bulkhead, leading to the bridge.

Except for a spell in the South Atlantic, these gangways were continuously under water. The fuel charge pipe was somewhere in the centre, and I always had to give the Chief a hand in screwing in a pipe in order to top off the diesel in the engine room without too much water pouring in. Our tug had a tough time and did everything except make somersaults. Our Captain withdrew very soon; so did the Second Mate, but I talked him into the job at hand again and he really did his best not to be seasick. Having left at noon, we were across Dover at midnight. I had not been off the bridge at all except for a dash to the loo. Our A.B.s were good and did not show any sign of weakness.

I was just contemplating trying to get the Captain to do a spell, when the Chief came on the bridge, telling me that he could not stand any longer on his feet; secondly water was pouring through the skylights and the steering engine was on the point of breaking down; thirdly he needed some new special injectors. So we turned round and back we went, arriving in the Hook by the afternoon. The Captain was on the bridge when the Pilot boarded us and he told him a dramatic story of our misfortunes so far. A telegram was sent to New York for the injectors, which were seemingly only available from the States. They arrived two days later by airmail. The Captain, after a chat with the Chief, decided to leave that evening, so off we went again. The weather was awful, but who cares, the Captain went straight to his bunk and the Second Mate was really flaked out this time.

Chief kept me company that night. He said his motor driver was good, and I will never forget that night. Our craft stood on its head, on its tail-end, rolled at the same time, shook itself like a dog coming out of the water; besides all that, there was a full moon, which shone a weird light on this crazy spectacle. Fortunately it had stopped raining, so I could see where I was going. Chief and I assisted A.B.s taking a turn at the wheel, but we agreed that after eight hours of this, and having covered about twenty miles, we should take shelter till the weather improved a bit. I decided that Flushing would be the answer as we were just ten miles off it. In the early grey morning we spotted a pilot boat and he told us to follow him, as that would be the wisest thing to do.

This time I was dead beat and as soon as we had tied up alongside a British trawler twice our size, I went to bed and was out cold for the next sixteen hours. The Captain did not seem in the least surprised that we were in Flushing; he just talked more than ever about all the gales he had weathered. It was at this time that the crew found a new name for him: "Aunt Betty," and they never ever referred otherwise to him. On the other hand Chief and I got along famously and fortunately neither of us suffered from seasickness, which was perhaps just as well.

I still want to mention one outstanding character, the oldest man on board, about sixty; our cook-cum-steward. No praise was high enough; he was simply excellent, clean and efficient, gave us the most gorgeous meals and plenty of it, completely out of place on this tug, more at home on a passenger liner, we thought, but ... to our advantage. Even under the wettest conditions and most wild captious behaviour of the craft, he served us with delicious hot meals. He was a surprise, but a very nice one.

We stayed in Flushing for the next few days, in company of over two dozen trawlers of diverse nationalities, small ones and large ones, till the weather abated sufficiently. The first three days it seemed to be worse till it blew a full scale gale, but apart from bobbing up and down and bouncing against each other with the most unholy noise, we were as snug as a bug in a rug. The first to leave were the large trawlers; some Icelandic, and gradually in the course of two days all were gone including us in the afternoon of the fifth day.

Even the Captain was about to do his turn of bridge duty though we were still tossed around considerably. He looked very pale for once and did not talk, which was quite a relief for us. On his watch he sat in his chair and smoked and dribbled. The weather improved and after Dover decreased to force 4/5. The Captain started talking again and as we noticed that the same story about a certain event changed from day to day, nobody paid any attention to it any more; even the Second Mate, who so far had looked at him with a certain respect, could hardly hide his amusement.

We passed Ushant and crossed the Bay without any undue fuss. We established a certain routine of four hours on and off, the Captain and the Second Officer always doing their watch together. I was used to going without a long sleep; it was even very pleasant, and though the deep ocean swell and the one caused by the local winds made the movement quite unpredictable and rather unexpected, we all got used to it and did not notice it any longer, except at meal times when everything slid over the table and it became rather a trick to eat soup. By the time that we passed Cote de Rojas, it became warmer and jackets were abandoned, long trousers packed away and shorts worn by day.

It was about that time that I began to think about the crossing after Las Palmas. I had served as a cadet on ships plying between Holland and South American harbours, even been through Patagonian Canals to Valparaiso, but I had never been in the West Indies, so I was rather curious where to head for and how long it would take us. I asked the Captain for THE CHART … "All we have left is the 'Approach to Las Palmas'." I could not believe my ears; perhaps he had misunderstood me. "Oh, no, none whatsoever; I did not think that we needed them. I told the office how well I knew those waters, and it saved money." I was more than flabbergasted, I was stunned, and I must have shown it, because he asked me what was wrong about that. "Well, you tell me how we set a course and distance for wherever we have to head for." "I never thought of that," he muttered, and looked more stupid than the village idiot.

I left him and went to have a chat with my friend the Chief and to come to a decision what to do about this. "Perhaps he likes us to follow the plan of Columbus, following a certain latitude till you hit a coast somewhere and ask the natives what next street to take," [he said].

"Listen, Chief, we must give him the fright of his life, he fully deserves that. Apart from that, I am fairly certain in my mind that we can get some kind of Admiralty Chart in Las Palmas, also a List of Lights, etc; if not, a Pilot Chart will have to do, available I think in the Harbour Office. They surely will have an old copy; they keep an eye on the weather there."

We went together to see a frightened Old Man. He really showed his age at that moment of time. "You have to send a cable to Head Office tell them of our plight and to dispatch some relevant charts by Air Mail, the excuse being that you left them behind by mistake. We are not leaving without those Charts." With that we left him to his silence. Believe it or not, but he did not say a word until we were anchored in the harbour five days later, and nobody felt sorry for him as far as we knew. Pilotage was not compulsory here, and by noon we had anchored near the only jetty, the one used by Shell for bunkering.

A very quiet Captain joined us for lunch (he always had his meals in his cabin for some obscure reason). He asked what he should put in his telegram to Head Office. We told him of our suggestions, and one saw him visibly come to life once again. He was so relieved that for once he was without words and left – he must have been on the verge of a nervous breakdown. Soon after, a representative from the Agents came alongside and told us to move straight away to the jetty for bunkering, which in our case was swapping empty barrels for full ones and taking on fresh water. As far as he could see, we could stay alongside till we sailed, so I told the crew that they could go ashore till midnight and to try to stay sober.

The Chief and I went ashore to try to find the British Consul and found that it was our ship's chandler, a very friendly and nice middle-aged gentleman. We told him of our plight, just saying that we seemed to have mislaid the chart when collecting them in Holland. "Well, that is not as easy as you think, but I will contact the Harbourmaster's office." He asked us to come back at five, then he would certainly know one way or another, and with that promise we left Mr Pringle.

We stopped a taxi and had a lovely bargaining session as is customary in these parts of the world. He wanted £5 as a starter, I offered 10/- and we met midway and agreed on 30/-. That was for a trip round the island, right up towards the top of the highest hill, where Mr Pringle had told us there was a good teahouse. Not many tourists went there, because the liners never stayed more than two or three hours in port. And it was indeed a grand tour, and the teahouse gave a splendid view over the whole island and harbour. We enjoyed it tremendously and were back at the Consul at five o'clock. He met us at the door, and had no chart. So far a blank, but he had heard of some retired mariner who might help us out. "Don't give up hope yet," he said, and invited us for dinner at the British Club, a splendid affair where Royalty had dined and wined. Churchill held court here for two days during the War, Mr Pringle told us. The dinner was a huge success: lobster salad to start with, a splendid steak and asparagus, peach melba to finish off with, coffee on the veranda where all those important personages had had their coffee and brandy. Mr Pringle was indeed a perfect host and we showed him our great appreciation: "I am a bachelor and enjoy my food and good company," and with this exchange of compliments he saw us back to our Tub.

The crew had not returned by midnight, only the Second Mate who had been ashore with the motor driver: "We saw them, the whole drunken lot, making a hell of a row in the Harbour Terrace Café with two Guardia-civil keeping a wary eye on them; they will surely sober up in the calaboose."

At six next morning a man from the Agents came on board to tell us that a tanker was arriving at eight and would we please "impshi" (move quickly).

The crew had not returned, so the Captain suggested that he would handle the telegraph. Chief offered to go down by himself. The Second Mate was told to stand by the anchor and I went ashore to throw off the ropes and spring, and jump back on board (fortunately no current here), pulled in all and went to the bridge. I manoeuvred her gently to a suitable spot out of the way and we anchored there.

We were having a leisurely breakfast when Mr Pringle arrived with a roll, what we presumed was a chart. And so it was. He rolled it out and I looked at it. At first glance I could not make out what was strange about it. Then it dawned on me: it was a Spanish Chart and calculated on the Meridian of Cadiz. It covered the whole western side of Europe, including the Faroes, the British Isles, the Spanish and Portuguese possessions: the Cape Verde Islands, the Canaries and Tenerife and the Gold Coast. "I am sure in a big house in Gourock one can do something with this." He also handed me an

Admiralty Book of Lights on the West Indies and a Pilot Chart of same, date of issue: 1898.

Having only particulars, such as declination and variation, based on Greenwich, we had to add 6° 7_ to all figures of longitude. Also my whole knowledge of figuring a position was calculated on the Meridian of Greenwich, so I had to alter the Chart.

The largest longitude on the Western side was 36° 13_, converted to 42° 30_ W. The latitude did not matter, of course. I found that I had to head for Trinidad, to a lighthouse called P. Galera at 54° 37_ W., 10° 55_ N.

In order to be able to do that on the chart, I had to go to the East side and 13° 20_ L., 16° 00_ N., from where I could set a course to P. Galera at 54° 37_ W., 10° 55_ N. Total distance 2800 miles, course 248°.

Of course I did not see all that at the breakfast table, but gradually in the quiet of the bridge. But I knew that Mr. Pringle had done us a great service. We gave him a stone jar of Dutch gin which he was delighted with. Our crew came back, looking like something the cat had brought in. I did not say anything about it; they would be doing their best.

We left at noon, and having one course to steer after we left the Isles, we fell into an easy routine of four on and eight off, the Second or Captain not being able to do much harm till we reached, with corrections, P. Galera. I had calculated ten days and five hours and so it turned out, with time correction: we saw the light ten days later at 1.00 a.m. The trip through the West Indies was a picnic, but I never trusted the Captain's knowledge, and just as well, because the second night after leaving Trinidad, our course was 35° out. He was heading for Jamaica or heaven knows where. I could not even be angry. After all, he was the Captain.

Note

For anybody interested, here is the title of the Chart: 'Carta del Océano Atlántico Septentrional [En dos Hojas] Hoja 1: Costas del Europa y África' (Chart of the Northern Atlantic Ocean [In two Sheets] Sheet 1: Coasts of Europe and Africa) – Depósito Hidrográfico. – MADRID 1898.

I am writing this fifty years later, and I am sure that Bernard never told the Superintendent the story of the trip. – M. Soep

15

South America – Home and Away

On arrival in Venezuela in 1948, Bernard started as a Chief Officer on the small tankers ferrying oil from the wells to the refinery in Cardon, after which it was exported.

After a short time he was promoted to Captain and had his own ship. He thoroughly enjoyed the work, sailing to different small places round Lake Maracaibo and meeting the native people working at the wells and seeing the little villages where the families lived. He spoke fluent Spanish, which was a great advantage, both with the crews and ashore. It was made very clear that Spanish was the language of the country and all foreigners were expected to speak it. I was asked to take lessons before I joined my husband. In August 1949 my young son John and I arrived in Cardon – what a relief, and how wonderful to be met by Bernard and to be a family again.

We came to Cardon, which was a Shell Complex with a variety of types of house for all types of employees. All needs were provided for, such as a shop, club, school, medical facilities. John played with various children and was soon talking in Spanish and Dutch.

The name Cardon means desert, and it hardly ever rained. Water was brought by tanker and there was still quite a bit of oil in the water, even though the tankers had been washed, so we filtered the water with the aid of cotton wool in a sieve, leaving the tap running slowly for a considerable time. Drinking water was supplied by distilling seawater and then putting it through a filter.

We settled in to life with a variety of folk of different nationalities, but mainly Dutch, British and of course Venezuelan. To speak Spanish was essential. It was their country, and it was up to visitors to speak their language.

Bernard was sent up to New York where several tank landing craft, which had been bought from the British Government, were being converted into small tankers suitable for use on parts of the lake. The trips down the coast from New York to Venezuela were rather hazardous, due to repeated breakdowns and some storms, and once requiring to take shelter to have damage repaired as the particular craft had sprung a leak

Bernard was made up to Pilot, which entailed bringing the big tankers to ports in and out of the area, and he thoroughly enjoyed the work. This meant a move to Maracaibo.

The life there was very different. It was a big town with big houses and small groups of bungalows in pleasant grounds. There was a club and swimming pool, which was well used, and films shown outside several nights per week.

It was here that our second son Roger was born. We enjoyed the life and had many good friends.

We had some very interesting holidays up in the mountain regions. The roads were quite an adventure; the Americans were building new highways, and we met frequent landslides and patches of deep mud. The scenery was wonderful and the people so helpful and friendly.

Some time later the government decided to get rid of as many foreigners as possible, and as Bernard was the last in, his contract was not to be renewed. So home again to Gourock in the spring of 1953.

When we came home, a job was offered to Bernard with the Halal Shipping Company, which entailed going abroad again for three years to work in the Eastern Mediterranean, Suez Canal and Red Sea area of the Middle East, which was a long time to be away from the family, I felt.

As my father had died, my mother was on her own in a big house in Gourock, with the exception of her housekeeper, Louie, who had been with her since I was a little girl. She persuaded the boys and myself to stay with her, as my brother George had taken a flat in Glasgow. He had been asked by Tom Weir, Douglas Scott and Tom McKinnon, who were all members of the Scottish Mountaineering Club, to join them on an expedition to Nepal for some months, and he could only accept if I stayed with mother, as she had never lived alone, even for a night. John started at school, and Roger was just a baby of eight months.

That was a long three years with two small boys. Mother and Louie enjoyed the children, but when I said, "No," to Roger it did not have much effect since, being the youngest, he was spoiled by both of them. Also I was sent over now and then to help my eldest sister, Jane, the Burgh Librarian in Dunfermline; that did not help either.

Maybe that's why I was persuaded to join the Guides?

16

Guides

Around the time we returned from Venezuela, a neighbour persuaded me to join the Toast Mistresses Club, where we were encouraged to speak in public. I made some good friends and as a result was persuaded to help with our church Guides, the 1st Gourock Company. I was informed by the Gourock District Commissioner that I did not have to do much – but she did not know me!

I went down to the meeting and about ten girls were round a table with the Lieutenant studying a book of knots. They were learning how to tie a packer's knot. Well, I had my Boatswain's badge and knew how to tie the knots behind my back. A number of the girls were meaning to leave but then decided to stay a bit longer to learn some more knots! It was a wonderful experience, and I treasure the memories of those years, all the fun and adventures we had, particularly at camp. I went with two local Guiders, Mary Boyd and Vera Macdonald, on a training course to gain a camp licence, which we achieved, but what an undertaking!

I set to and arranged our first camp at Hunters Quay in the grounds owned by the Camp Adviser for Argyll.

The camps were always during the Greenock Fair holidays, but as Roger was too young for Scout camp he had to come with me. He slept in my tent but spent the days in one of the patrols along with the girls and learned many skills, which were very useful when he finally reached Scouts. To this day there is still much amusement when Marion White, Roger's Patrol Leader, still tells him what to do whenever she meets him.

I managed to persuade some fathers to form a Patrol and they happily carried all the equipment and other baggage to McGinn's bus or lorry. They were mostly Clyde Pilots, and they were rewarded with a fine lunch when they visited the camp on visitors' day. The bus took us to the site, but the Patrol Leaders went a day ahead with me, and the rest followed the next day. We only pitched the store tent and our own. The Guides had to do their own work when they arrived. We camped every year and twice went to Dunagoil Bay on the Island of Bute. It was wonderful beside the beach, and we had a lifesaver, so we could bathe. The Patrols always had a day expedition entirely on their own. It was very special, and the leaders were totally responsible to me – you would not be allowed to do that today. Bernard was at home while all this was going on and took all the phone calls from some anxious parents who were suitably reassured that all was well despite the weather. Our dog Judy was also part of the team and had an uncanny sense of knowing if there was an intruder on the site, despite frequent visits of girls to the latrines. The campsite was located in an area of special archaeological merit and we held our Guides Own service up on one of the hillocks nearby. We had a total of seven camps, every year.

I used the Patrol System which was the basis of the early Scouts and Guides started by Lord and Lady Baden Powell so long ago. As the Guider I was aided by my Lieutenants in training the leaders, and they in turn trained their Guides. We were fortunate in having Nethered Training Centre near Peebles where both Guiders and Patrol Leaders could be trained. My visit there had resulted in me being told to gain my camp licence and take my own Guides and family if necessary. Taking the family was not a problem as we were already used to camping holidays.

There were two types of training for the Guides, one to aid them to learn activities which would enable them to help or run a meeting and two others for helping to gain camp skills for the campers badge and finally for the camp permit. This allowed them to take their Guides on their own for a few days, as long as they were camped within sight of a responsible adult. For us that was Willie Baird of Levanne Farm, Gourock. He also allowed us to keep equipment in a barn. On some Saturdays we went to a field near woods and cooked our lunch. In this way the leaders gained more skills and learned to be more responsible and able to help plan and run meetings and camp activities.

It was wonderful, and after I finished my ten years as Division Commissioner I had some lovely letters, saying how those experiences helped them in life. I found the responsibility that I had as a young Guide was a great help to me in later years when nursing in the army. I have always used the Patrol System in my work. I still use it now!

The most special thing that we achieved as a Division, when I was Commissioner, was the effort everybody put into the building of the Bettyburn Camp Hut. We had the most fantastic help from all official departments and the Youth Committee, and especially from Sir Guy Shaw Stewart who lent us the ground for as long as we wanted. Unfortunately, it has recently had to be demolished because of housing, which was sad. I wrote the story for the Annual Report and all the kind helpers were sent a copy and thanked, including Mr Paxton, Managing Director of the Greenock Dockyard Company, and his friend John Tweedle, who was the joiner involved in the construction.

Guides worldwide celebrate 'Thinking Day' on 22 February each year and give funds for those in need. In the early days Guides of certain different religions required to mark this occasion on separate Sundays. Bishop Stephen McGill gladly gave his permission and Monsignor Kinsella helped arrange the first joint service in Greenock Town Hall. I shall never forget the very special moment of standing on the platform and watching all my girls marching side by side with their Colours to be received by the Minister and Priest. Bishop Stephen McGill did so much to get rid of the absurd differences and so it continues today. He was followed by Bishop Mone and Father Tom of Gourock who is now a Monsignor and has been our County Chaplain for many years.

17

Rankin Maternity Hospital

After a very long three years Bernard returned in 1956, but the ship had broken down and he was towed up the Clyde. I managed to get aboard with the Customs Officer that night. Next day I took the boys to meet their Dad. Three years was a long time. John was very shy. Roger was picked up by a big Arab; he did not like that and when we were in the cabin he just stood and said very firmly, "I am Roger," with a fierce look which clearly indicated, "Do not touch me!" After a while the novelty of being a dad wore off, and Bernard was told by Roger on one occasion that "he could go back to his ship and take his big wireless with him". That settled things for Bernard; he decided that he would never leave his family again.

I had taken a furnished house, till we knew what we were going to do. Eventually Bernard was advised to go into partnership, and the Mora Company was formed at Battery Park in Greenock. Mora made various designs of manual control boards for many companies and organisations. The application of moraine on documents, plans, charts or pictures replaced glass when heated under pressure and was particularly useful for ships. The Matron and tutor of Rankin Maternity Hospital came and wanted a control board to be able to view the progress of the students. Bernard must have remarked that I was a midwife, and – as they badly needed one – I was asked to an interview at Rankin Maternity Hospital with the Matron, Miss Dees. On 5 January 1965 I returned to my career.

The Assistant Matron Miss MacMackin took me to the postnatal ward and introduced me to the relief Sister. She looked at this rather elderly nurse and remarked that I could take the temperatures for the evening check ups, handed me the jar of thermometers and the report book, and told me to do the evening checks – this at 10.30 a.m. The ward Sister on duty next day and I had a very happy spell in ward one, and we are still good friends to this day. I had to have an extensive refresher course with Miss Black, the tutor, and some consultants so that I could be re-registered with the Scottish Midwives Board.

I started in the labour ward, and I was useful because they did their own theatre days and I had my Army theatre certificate. I was working part time, but some time later I was promoted to Sister and given charge of the antenatal ward. I was delighted and could arrange my own hours as long as I did them. Then, quite a number of changes took place. The consultant, Dr Baxter, who had been in charge for a considerable time, was retiring, and there were two wards each with their own consultant with antenatal and postnatal patients in separate rooms. Dr Murray had ward one and Dr Hodge had ward two, which was mine. There was also Dr

Barr, who was the Senior Consultant for Renfrewshire, and Dr Martin, who had his own clinic for patients in one area of Greenock. Dr Murray had Gourock and the west end of Greenock, and Dr Hodge looked after the east end of Greenock, Port Glasgow, Rothesay and Dunoon, and then we had a new Matron, Miss Aitken, who was full of new ideas.

Before long I was put on night duty in charge of the hospital, though the labour ward was not my problem unless they needed help with babies. As we did not have a consultant-led special baby care unit, any babies needing specialist care had to be sent to the Queen Mother's Hospital in Glasgow. There was a small incubator which had its own oxygen supply and was kept heated to the correct temperature, making it ready for use at all times. I personally checked this equipment for serviceability as soon as I came on duty. If it was needed, a nurse was dispatched by taxi to Glasgow with the incubator and baby. This was very good experience for me. During that time Matron took me to the meetings for the tutors and as a result I was given the opportunity to take an eight-month day release course for a Clinical Teachers Certificate at Simpson's Maternity Hospital, Edinburgh, where the senior tutor was Miss Grant, the most superb teacher who inspired and encouraged me to do things that I would not have thought possible.

I was on night duty at this time and was given a night off per week to allow me to attend the class. It meant leaving on the 6.30 a.m. train and not getting back to Greenock until 8.00 p.m.. I don't think that I ever worked so hard, but I was determined to succeed. The theory of anatomy and physiology required much revision, and that exam was taken early. To my surprise I came top of the class; the younger ones thought that they would be able to remember the details without having to swot. I had been such a short time in the labour ward and felt that I was in need of tuition in that field. Every week Miss Grant gave us a paper to write, and the questions were very advanced.

My mother had taken very ill at this time, so I took extra unpaid leave and sat up with her most of the night, and I studied and studied. Once the topic was antenatal investigations and treatments, which was my specialty, and consequently I was able to write pages on the subject. Miss Grant's marking was tough, and this time she remarked that obviously I had done a lot of research. "No," was the reply, "I experience all these things every day in my ward." We had to do a thesis, and I chose the 'unmarried mother'. I visited the local centre and discovered that the situations I met in Greenock were of great use.

The exam came, including the practical – having a patient and a student midwife to teach. I imagined I was in my own ward, and got so carried away that when I had finished I thanked the student and let her go, and then I remembered the very senior tutor and the consultant who were sitting nearby looking somewhat surprised as a result of me having dispatched the subject of the exam – but never mind, I passed.

When I got back to work and my ward I found it so very satisfactory to be able to teach my students on the job. When they moved on after a spell I felt that they were capable. I just revelled in my ward and teaching the students on the job. I remembered the way at Barts when we each had a large chart that had to be filled in by every ward Sister, a tick when we had been taught and a cross when we were proficient.

Nurses' training has changed since these days and I feel that they do not have nearly enough bedside teaching today. There could be more, shorter courses with less detail for ward Sisters.

Miss Aitken secured the post of Matron at Rotten Row Maternity Hospital, Glasgow, and consequently a new young person came. Then the clinical teacher retired, and Miss Black eventually persuaded me to apply for the vacancy. She said she needed my enthusiasm, but I told her that I could not work without it and that she might have cause for regret.

Rankin was a very fine hospital and far ahead of many others. Midwives had to attend refresher courses every two years and there were opportunities to attend seminars. While at these seminars, if I asked questions I was always asked where I came from – they were surprised when I said Rankin, as we were far ahead of many other hospitals at that time. What Rotten Row had one month we had soon after.

To my surprise, when Matron was going on leave for two weeks she left me in charge, but certainly I was delighted. Then, just when I thought that I was safely back in my ward, Matron and Dr Murray had another idea; the Sister who had run the clinics for about seventeen years was retiring and they wanted changes.

It was decided that Soep could do it. No way was I interested, but they exerted considerable pressure. I was to be moved from my ward to reorganise the clinics and to set up parent craft classes. I suggested that we should try it for six months, and if it was not a success I could return to my ward. That was accepted. But I was given a big carrot. I could travel anywhere in Scotland and do exactly what I liked! No need to ask for anyone's permission! Certainly I could not refuse such a generous offer with such wonderful conditions.

I was allowed to choose my staff, and that made everything just wonderful. And my staff midwife was Ruth Gillies, who had been a student in my ward and then a staff midwife. My first trip was to Stirling Maternity Hospital as it was clinic day and it was only for new patients. In Stirling, they all saw the sister who ran the Parent Craft Classes where breastfeeding was encouraged. This was a *very* good idea, and so back I went to see how we would arrange it. My chosen staff midwife had been a student and had worked on my ward. Our clinics were held in different places; the two main ones were held in The Royal in the centre of Greenock. But I wanted it to be in Rankin, where the patients would be delivered. The idea was to have all the new patients together with the appointments staggered throughout the day, if necessary, with midwives, students, a health visitor and a social worker available. It was held in a spare room in ward two, and we could provide cups of tea or coffee.

We had the case notes all ready the day before and we could take as long as necessary; we hoped that as many as possible would agree to make a date for the parent craft. There was a big clinic in Boglestone, Port Glasgow with Dr Margaret Lamb in charge and local nurses and health visitors running it. I was allowed to use my car for all these expeditions, and Friday at the 'Port' was always a special, happy day. We ran the parent craft classes, including the relaxation, as I had been trained in that at the Radcliffe Hospital in Oxford by the famous Grantly Dick Reed.

At Dr Murray's insistence she gave me a clinic to myself with patients selected by her. I was on my own but if necessary could ask her advice. She said that that was what my training was for and it was not being used. The clinics were happy and successful and I had my own auxiliaries as well to assist me, who could inform us of the patient's worries or concerns if required. The auxiliaries were an essential part of the team. Strangely enough some years later midwives are running antenatal clinics in doctors surgeries.

I required to go into hospital for a small repair job of my own and Dr Murray allowed me to determine when I could leave my staff. With a staff of two midwives for the clinics we now had and the parentcraft classes, which were now more readily acceptable to the husbands and the labour ward staff, things were running on such an even keel that getting away was a lot easier for all concerned. Some months later when I returned, and to her surprise having obeyed Dr Murray's instructions, the team were all doing so well that I felt that I was almost redundant.

By now the teaching department was in need of a clinical teacher as there had been a retirement. Very reluctantly I agreed to take it on. I was sixty-two and had to retire in three years. Fortunately Miss Black let me do as I liked and we had a happy team. A few days after I had started, the hospital had the usual two yearly visit from the Central Midwives Board. So I had to answer for the department that I had just left. To my amazement it was Miss Grant the tutor that I had on the course. She was so interested and delighted in what we were doing with regard to our clinics and class and said that she was going to pass on the scheme to other units in Scotland. What a compliment!

I enjoyed my time in the teaching department and had the students training for R.G.N., including men. When this was introduced, the midwives were very disapproving. We had eight at a time; there could be two men amongst them. On one particular occasion two men had missed their training and were due to sit their final exam. I had warned the patients and that was no problem, except that the two students were rather alarmed. However, the hospital was very busy and they were thrown in at the deep end and soon forgot the question of modesty and did very well, even dealing with deliveries and breast-feeding in the G.P. Unit. I enjoyed those eight weeks.

Rankin was a very happy place for staff as well as patients, and there were grand parties at Christmas for patients, their families and also staff. The staff had two separate evening functions, one for trained staff and the other for the rest, when we waited on them. In the old

Rankin the students and some staff had rooms upstairs. We had a considerable number from Ireland, where they had trained in strict hospitals, so consequently enjoyed the freedom in Rankin. Eventually Rankin had to move to the I.R.H., as there had to be a resident anaesthetist for those wishing epidural pain relief; however, the unit still was referred to as the Rankin.

I made so many good friends. I still meet many in the various groups I have been involved with since. When I retired from the Rankin at the end of October 1978 I had a grand tea party and was given a tumble drier, which was my husband's choice, while he was given a coffee maker. Mr Baker, the Principal of the Nurses' Training School, came too, and passed some very nice comments and later invited me to give a presentation and hand out the certificates at the next graduation ceremony.

18

Glenfield Medical Aid Home

My final retirement had come; now for some relaxation. We did some visiting and my old Matron told me that I was too young to retire and that Greenock needed a Hospice. I put that at the back of my mind. One day I came home to be told by my husband that he had had a phone call from a lawyer saying that the Matron of the Medical Aid Home, Glenfield had taken a stroke and could I please take over. Bernard explained he had accepted on my behalf. Well, that was the end of my retirement for some time! Up to Glenfield, and I had no option. I was also expected to cater for the forty-two residents. The nearest I had come to this was catering for twenty-four guides for a week. When I was first married I had to phone my mother to ask how to cook potatoes!

My first instinct was to rush to Rankin, where my story was greeted with howls of laughter. Fortunately, the Catering Manager for Larkfield and Rankin was in the kitchen, and he gave me menus with quantities for forty-two. I returned the next day to borrow some necessary nursing equipment. The Ladies Committee were very sympathetic, and I was quite sure that the idea had been the Chairman's, whom I had known as a young girl in Gourock. I suppose as she had witnessed her neighbour's antics going to camps she felt I ought to be able to cope. The next person who welcomed me was Mr Lynn, who was the member of the committee responsible for the home. He was so kind and was in every day and always available on the phone He realised that I had been thrown in at the deep end and there had been no handover. The next stroke of luck was a phone call from Sandra Blair asking if she could come and help. A quick phone call to the lawyer, and permission was granted. Of course she was a trained nurse as well as being a Guide. During the phone call the lawyer reminded me that the salary I was being paid would require to be rather modest, as after all I was working for a charity, which could not afford a large figure. I almost hastened to remind him that unlike the Matron, I was not living in.

The Medical Aid Society was a longstanding charity which had a home for usually retired folk, mostly women who were in need of comfortable and affordable accommodation; the home had moved several times but had been in Bedford Street for a good many years.

Glenfield was a lovely big old house with spacious bedrooms and sitting rooms as well as good bathrooms, sluices etc. Downstairs there was an adequate dining room, additional bedrooms and the most inadequate kitchen one could imagine. There were forty-two residents in all. A new wing, later to be called the Drummond Wing, had very recently been opened and was still taking in residents. There were 12 bedrooms, 6 on each floor with a couple of bathrooms, a small kitchenette and a beautifully decorated sitting room with views of the gardens and the cricket grounds next door. The residents were able to bring small items of their own personal furniture with them, which gave them a degree of independence.

I foresaw problems could arise when the residents were in need of additional levels of attention; when this was required discussion took place between the doctors and the families before they were moved to the main wing, where facilities were more suitable. The residents all had their own medication as if they were in their own home, although this was kept locked away in a special cupboard in the duty room. This was a perfect nightmare to deal with. A pharmacist from Greenock came once a week and the doctor prescribed for each resident.

There was really a lot of nursing that needed to be done, and that was not possible with only one trained nurse on duty at a time. In the main sick ward there were two ladies with bedsores the like of which I had never seen during my nursing career. The staff were in the habit of calling the residents by their Christian names. One very elderly lady had been a Matron, and I assertively corrected the nursing auxiliary and said, "This is Miss X, who was a Matron." I will never forget the look of delight on the lady's face. All that has changed nowadays.

The catering was another nightmare. Food seemed to be delivered on various days; the cook was quite inadequate, and so were the facilities. As this was November and Christmas was fast approaching I was terribly worried about Christmas dinner. However, another good friend from the church, who was of course a Guider, and – more importantly – a trained cook in charge of school catering, said she would be on holiday and offered to have everything ready just to heat on the day. This arrangement worked very well as I was already committed to be on holiday over that period with the family in Carradale; as it turned out Sandra was happy to cover the New Year, her husband playing the part of Santa Claus.

After Christmas, I wanted to see what happened round the clock. There was a trained nurse who came on duty at 7.00 p.m. and worked on till about 11.00 p.m. and then went to bed on call, getting up in time to give the medicines and ready to hand over at 7.30 a.m. to the day staff. This was a good way of covering as they could go home and look after the family with no need to go to bed.

At one point new fire doors were being fitted and the joiner, Mr John Goodlet, enquired if I would consider a post for his wife. Maureen started with us a few weeks later and remained in Glenfield as a Senior Auxiliary until becoming the Care Officer in Bagatelle Court in 1997. Around the same time I was invited to attend the final sessions of the monthly committee meetings, and over a period I was able to persuade them to improve the salaries of the four Senior Auxiliaries, as I knew they had been offered alternative employment with enhanced wages but were too loyal to make the move.

I asked the Manager in charge of the Heath Board for help with equipment and was told firmly that we were not part of the Health Service, but I insisted that my residents were entitled to the same lifestyle as if they were in their own homes. There was a Mr Johnstone, a very kind and longsuffering gentleman, who told me to go to Glasgow to Yorkhill Hospital where I would find what I wanted.

Another kind friend, our next-door neighbour Ken Smith, had a Land Rover and was pleased to embark on this latest adventure. We were made very welcome, and there were vast numbers of mauve and white striped uniforms. They said that those that we did not need would be thrown out. A thrifty Girl Guide just said thank you and took the lot! What fun we had when we returned to the home. "Help yourselves and alter them to fit." Nowadays I do not see that colour.

I had discovered from Sandra that she was interested in continuing in the job but needed time to organise her family. Now I felt that I had a target and could look forward to a final retirement as I had stipulated that two years was the maximum I was prepared to remain in post. I decided to ask for help and the committee contacted the local Health Board in Paisley, who duly dispatched the Deputy Head of Nursing, who when she saw our problems was horrified and immediately authorised the supply of the necessary equipment. Mr Johnstone in Bagatelle, which was at that time the administrative centre for the Health Board in Greenock, gave me great assistance in procuring additional furniture, fittings and equipment that was not going to be needed in the new hospital. One of the first calls, however, was once more to my good friends associated with Rankin, and via my contacts in the laundry I was able to increase our depleted stock of sheets by being notified to keep drawing stock until my shelves were full. The new Inverclyde Royal Hospital was opening and equipment not required was offered to other hospitals, after which we could have our pick. I went to see the sterilising unit beside Rankin, and as it happened the lady on duty was our postman's wife. She gave us lots of sterile dressings etc. which she had been told to dump before the new hospital opened, so our shelves were filled once more with much needed essentials – what more could I ask? Around this time I also fell heir to a large wooden cupboard, which was ideal as a replacement for the little box type receptacle that up until this time had secured the medication – this large cupboard became the medicine chest in the duty room. I then asked the doctor and the pharmacist if they could get rid of the individual medicines we had on hand and replace them with the stock bottles I was used to dealing with. Years later I was informed that this system was illegal – more of which later.

In the meantime a new chairman was appointed, and he came to introduce himself, Mr Duncan Drummond of Drummonds Packaging. What a truly wonderful person. We were just asked to say what we wanted and what we wanted him to do. He was concerned to hear about our problems. My first need was to be able to make up case sheets, starting with treatment sheets on which medication would be ordered and signed. I was given permission to go to Rae's, the local printers, and get all the stationery that I needed. One of our night Sisters who was an expert in calligraphy did all the headings, our Doctor dealt with the treatment sheets gladly and I had a fascinating time writing up the histories of all the residents, found in a large, very old leather bound book which had been unearthed from a cupboard. It is now amongst the archives.

We were still in great need of a cook, and through a friend we heard of someone who was running her own small hotel, who for her own reasons wished to move from Argyll to the Greenock area. She was a great success, and she managed to have the kitchen and pantry brought up to date with a freezer, dishwasher and many other improvements, and of course supplied us with wonderful cooking and baking.

All this time I was well supported by the Ladies Committee, who raised money and provided numerous decorations and curtains for all the rooms, crockery for the dining room and many extras for the residents. We had outings in the summer, and those that were able attended functions and concerts at the Arts Guild Theatre, the committee members using their own cars as the transport. One highlight at the end of evening activities was tea and toast round the fireside in the drawing room – a good time was had by all.

A while before retiral my grapevine informed me that the old Larkfield Hospital was about to be demolished, so off I went on the scrounge to see if I could procure the stainless steel sink from the old orthopaedic ward and a washhand basin for the Sick

Room. Mr Johnstone told me to take the young architect Willie Charles and remove what we wanted, with a stipulation that whatever was removed had to be out of the building by the Friday – we were very successful, we did not needed telling twice; we filled McEwan's lorry to overflowing and what was not needed at the time was stored until later. The surplus ended up in the Third World

Some weeks before the March A.G.M. I received a phone call from the Chairman of the Health Board in Paisley who asked if he could pay a quick visit to Glenfield as he was to be the main speaker at the A.G.M. and wished to gather some background before writing his address. On his arrival after the usual welcome he proceeded to investigate every corner of the building and was very complimentary at what he found. Finally we arrived in the duty room and taking the keys from my pocket I unlocked my special medicine cupboard, whereupon he roared with laughter and said, "Of course you know it's illegal," to which I replied, "Fine, you take the keys and I can go home." He replied "I think it is brilliant, just carry on," which we did until the two nursing homes went on the Boots System some years later.

Eventually, my two years were up, and as there was a fine Sister at hand to take over I knew that things were going to a safe pair of hands. On my last day I was trying to finish a few things and I could not seem to get hold of any staff; they just said that they were busy. Suddenly I was told that there was a need for me to go to the sitting room. With my cap at an angle and feeling

221

very untidy I went as requested. The whole staff were there, and Bernard too! I asked what he was doing, and he replied that he had been kidnapped. There was a beautiful cake and flowers handed over by a special elderly resident. I also received a lovely gold watch from all of them

I will always be so grateful to the Medical Aid Society for so many kindnesses. In addition, the working environment was such that we were all a happy bunch to the extent that our families managed to get involved from time to time as well.

Bernard was always on hand to help in any way possible, particularly at Christmas and other parties – he was the life and soul. Some time later Bernard was very unwell with cancer and we were moving to a more suitable flat. Sandra said that he was to come and stay at Glenfield until the place was in proper order. Later still my sister was a resident for over ten years and latterly due to brain damage she was very difficult and wild. The care she had was absolutely wonderful.

The committee persuaded us to put our names down for Bagatelle Court, and here I am happily settled and still spoilt with Sandra and Maureen near at hand.

Did I say retired? No such thing. A tap on the shoulder by Dr Kennedy, "Marion, now the Hospice."

19

Ardgowan Hospice

It was January 1981. I had just retired from Glenfield Medical Aid Home when Dr John Kennedy told me that now it was the hospice where I was needed. I was welcomed on to the Steering Committee.

The old Greenock Eye Infirmary was to close, and the work would be transferred to the new Inverclyde Royal Hospital. One of the Staff Nurses, Mrs Hardcastle, felt that a hospice was needed and that this building might be suitable.

There had been contact with Prue Clench, in charge of the hospice in Bath, and she came here to advise and was very helpful. She explained that if we started with Macmillan Nurses we did not need a building, which would give us time to raise the necessary money. Contact was made with The Macmillan Fund, who were helping new hospices to be formed. They were prepared to provide the money to pay the builders, as long as we repaid as soon as we had raised sufficient funds. So the idea was launched.

A small nursing committee was formed which eventually consisted of Miss McLean, the Nursing Officer for the Community, Maris Roxburgh, Theatre Superintendent and myself.

McEwan was chosen as the builders, Mr George Gerrard as the surveyor and the architect was Mr Andrew Forbes.

A leading consultant was asked to advise; he came down from Glasgow and spoke to a large audience in The Greenock Town Hall. He recognised that there was much enthusiasm and told everyone to gather into groups from the several districts represented and then raise much money. Small groups became active in Greenock, Gourock, Port Glasgow, Kilmacolm, Skelmorlie and Langbank.

Permission had to be obtained from the Health Board, but first we had to raise a large sum of money by way of legal guarantors. I think we were told to produce £20,000 in two weeks. I started with a lawyer and an accountant to devise methods of obtaining the guarantees required, and eventually this was achieved within the time frame, which allowed us to start.

Eventually the nursing group got busy and we visited Strathcarron (the newest hospice) and had great help from them. When I was staying near Edinburgh I visited their hospices, both of which had started with beds, then day care, finally with the Macmillan Nurses in the community, although there had been considerable opposition from the community authorities. That was a great help for us as we were hoping to start with Macmillan Nurses, and we had invited the Superintendent of the community on to our nursing committee.

The need to raise money was urgent, and we all set to with a will. A huge jumble sale in St Mungo's Church

Hall was organised and then a street collection run by Margaret McDougall, using cans borrowed from The Red Cross; everyone joined in with great good humour.

I asked Tom Weir to come and help us by showing some of his slides. He was a great friend of my brother George Roger, and they were both past presidents of the Scottish Mountaineering Club. Tom started in a Church Hall and then we moved to The Arts Guild Theatre. That was repeated every two years with a final show, which was very special with the hall packed; £2,500 was raised. That was just before his 89th birthday; sadly he became ill and now is in a nursing home but is content, and enjoys visits from his friends.

Other fundraising efforts included numerous collections on the Western Ferries in May when English visitors were on holiday, Caledonian MacBrayne's from Wemyss Bay for Rothesay Highland Games, and Gourock for Cowal Highland Games. There were a great number of collectors who enjoyed themselves, especially those who had the early morning trip on the Western Ferries and were given coffee and bacon rolls.

A big event was Hospice Week in July when we had the whole area divided into districts, each with an organiser, with volunteers collecting in various streets. It was a huge operation and brought in a large amount of money. The generosity in all the areas was so splendid, particularly in the housing schemes.

Dr Kennedy was still the visionary behind us all, but then a council was formed with David Foggie (a lawyer) as Chairman, and two Macmillan Nurses were appointed. Both had been local Health Visitors and they were given an office in the local Health Centre. This established a first-rate service, and considerable interest built up with the community staff, which was grand, as this method of organisation ensured that we had no problems.

Once the Macmillan Nurses (Anne Billiemore and Ethel Paton) were established and patients were sent to Glasgow for treatment, which could be for five days per week over six weeks, it soon became obvious that we must try to help with our own transport. If the ambulances were used, the patients had to be ready any time after 8.30 a.m. and would return during the afternoon, delivering patients to different parts, which could mean arriving home after 5.00 p.m. The nursing group were asked to arrange transport.

As Bernard was an invalid by now, I did not wish to be away for long, so with a number of good friends and contacts I got busy and soon had a number of drivers who gladly joined, and it worked well once the Nurses allowed me to contact the patients direct. It was easy once we had a card system with times when the drivers were available and another list for local trips. The head Clyde pilot said that since he went to Glasgow every morning he could help, and again in the late afternoon to return.

The drivers were all paid an allowance to cover the cost of petrol. They were asked to hand in the trips' details and the mileage. My difficulty was with those who did not wish payment and I had to do the sums:

that was left to Bernard. If we were in difficulties the Hospital League of Friends were very helpful.

Our first Matron, Jean Galbraith, was appointed in August 1985 originally as Sister-in-charge. In that role, she became the visionary who developed a great number of the ideas for the services the hospice carries out to this day. Later she was promoted to Matron.

The next move was for the day care patients, and this meant the enlargement of the big sitting room extending into the garden, also the little room and balcony. The dining room and kitchen were finished, and Marks and Spencer's provided all the equipment, and Arnott's all the crockery; this was very generous.

Dr Kennedy was so happy walking round in his white coat and seeing his dream coming true.

It was necessary for someone to be able to man the telephone on New Years Day. I offered, and brought Bernard and our dog. John, and Margaret Kennedy joined us. We had a great time, despite the fact that I had to make the omelette in a large saucepan, as there was no special frying pan. This party will always be remembered, particularly by Margaret, as John died two weeks later from a heart attack while on a ferry on his way to visit an invalid friend.

Before the Day Care Centre was opened it was envisaged that we would need more volunteers, and a public meeting was held in James Watt College. The meeting was well attended, and over 160 people filled in volunteer application forms. All of these people were interviewed, given some training and then slotted into the different departments.

There were more drivers, fundraisers, people in the kitchen, housekeeping team, office staff, gardeners and of course carers for day care. The role of the volunteer remains vital to this day.

This new venture was opened by Tom Weir; I was so pleased that he had been asked. There was a Sister-in-charge with helpers and some trained volunteers. This meant that more patients could be cared for by spending one or two days in the hospice where they could be seen by the doctor, have meals, and get some of their problems dealt with. At midday there was a short service in the lovely chapel, which was a quiet place that was for anyone. One of the stained glass windows from the old eye infirmary was on the outside wall and another given by Dr Kennedy's family.

Other fundraising efforts were from shops, the first ones in Gourock, and then Greenock, and eventually also in Port Glasgow. The Health Boards throughout the whole country were meant to pay half the costs, but we did not reach that despite the amount of the savings they made as a result of the hospice care. The next idea David Foggie had was the possibility of beds. He called me in and told me to recruit someone to organise the transport. Handing me a book with the particulars of all the hospices in Britain, he told me to discover if we needed beds and if so how we could manage to achieve it.

Well, Margaret Black, my first driver, had offered to help with the transport. That was easily arranged, though I think she was a little surprised at the speed with which I took up her offer, but when she heard of my new instructions she understood.

This was some task, but encouraged by Bernard I set to. Actually, I think that he was quite pleased when the phone calls were much reduced. I studied the lists of hospices and eventually picked out seventeen. I hand-wrote letters to them, hoping that as it was a personal letter explaining our need and giving my qualifications it would be more effective. I had thirteen replies, all giving me as much detail as possible.

I made a kind of chart with the names of the hospices down the side and the requirements along the top. I thanked them all but picked out a few that were a little similar to us. I had more information from Plymouth, York and Belfast, and they were so keen to help us. It was very encouraging, just what we had experienced in Scotland. Finally I settled down to letters and telephone conversations with the Matron in Plymouth, and before long I had all the ideas ready to put in print.

During the next stage I had to have sessions with Jean to know what staff she needed and the grades. Full time was 42 hours per week, and if some were part time it was necessary to divide 42 into the part-time hours, and the result in the end was to appoint some part-time nurses. When all these calculations were made it appeared that one nurse to each patient was needed. It was fortunate that Bernard was able to supervise my arithmetic.

We had our council meeting, and it was decided to go to the next stage. Two teams were formed, David Foggie with Jean and George Gerrard to go away for three days to the South of England, and Sir James Watson Stewart, Ian Morrice and myself to go for two days to the North of England.

My elder son John came to stay with his dad.

These expeditions were useful, and we saw things that we did not want as well as those that would be useful. The next thing was to raise sufficient funds, so on we went, and there was such generosity in Inverclyde in all strands of society. Two of our staunch supporters were Sir Houston and Lady Lucinda Shaw Stewart at Ardgowan. Lady Lucinda was a Vice President of the hospice, and the family have always supported all the local community. At the beginning we were invited to have carol concerts at Ardgowan House before Christmas, on two separate nights, with the Da Capo choir singing. This has gone on for many years and becomes increasingly popular. During the interval Lady Lucinda gives those attending a sumptuous supper. There is always a raffle, and once again there is considerable generosity from companies and well-wishers.

Our eight-bedded hospice was ready. Some people thought that we should have had more beds, but apart from there being no room we had been advised that if we went above ten we would lose the family atmosphere.

The great day came, and H.R.H. Princess Margaret came to do the honours. She was so charming, speaking to all the staff and patients, and giving a word of encouragement to all the council members. In the evening we had a truly wonderful party for staff, council and all volunteers. I even met my drivers, whom I had only known over the telephone. What a difference this made to all the sufferers of cancer.

The doctors that followed John Kennedy were the retired Consultant Anaesthetist Dr Sam McKechnie with Dr Alison Clarke relieving him when necessary. She was an early member of the original support group and still does a great job with house to house and the ferry collections. Dr Alison Morrison has been in charge for many years. She was our Pain Control Specialist and also a consultant in the hospital. She has just left us for a very special job in Perth.

It was wonderful that patients could be looked after at all times. Duncan Macdonald was the Administrator at this time. There was also a team of chaplains from all denominations.

Things move on, and a grant was offered for a nurse to help newly diagnosed patients who were probably younger and still working and did not wish to come to the hospice. The nurse was appointed and the grant applied for to fund a new building.

Well, the miracle happened: George Gerrard had kept his eye on the big building that the Woman's Royal Voluntary Service used for various projects.

Suddenly Inverclyde Council was advised to demolish this building and offered it to the hospice: this was wonderful. They called a meeting and said that they were happy to give it, but more meetings were necessary. George was ready for that – they had been offered a large grant from the National Lottery Fund, but the papers had to be signed in a few days; I don't think Inverclyde Council had ever moved so fast. I believe they had their meeting that night.

So once again our local builder McEwan did the job, which was finished on time, and on 12 June 2001, the Access Centre was opened by H.R.H. Prince Charles. He was in his kilt and knew his subject. He did not want any ceremony and just went round, starting with the treatment area, and talked to patients and staff. He made a very good speech and talked to a little boy who had had treatment. He was clutching an electronic toy and when asked what it was he invited the Prince to have a go, which was accepted. After a short time, the Prince was told that he was not much good.

So time marches on, I resigned from the Hospice Council in 1997 after eighteen very happy years. I was delighted when my friend Fiona Cherry took my place. She trained at Barts Hospital, but years after me.

The time came for Jean's retirement and the problem was to find a new Matron. There were many advertisements and applications and eventually Dorothy McElroy, who had applied, asked to have a visit. When Jean met her she knew that the right person had been found. Then Dorothy took over, and they worked together for a few months.

What a happy time, and what a privilege it has been, and what friends I made. I am hopelessly spoilt, and I was given the most wonderful ninetieth birthday party with some of my family and guests that I was asked to invite. I asked many friends who had come to my help when I had been in need. Duncan McDonald, the Administrator, made very kind comments about my work at the hospice.

In 2005, it became necessary for the local Macmillan Nurses to undergo a name change. They must now be referred to as 'Ardgowan Community Nurse Specialists'.

This is directly linked to the fact that the Macmillan Nurses have *always* been funded by the Ardgowan hospice.

Now I have finished this story, and that could not have happened without many wonderful helpers. This should have been written when Bernard was still living and able to correct my mistakes. When I can get this published, the profits are to go to the Ardgowan hospice.

20

Finale for Bernard

Bernard retired in 1969, sold his business and cleared his debts. He was content. He never looked back. He had a busy retirement, like many other folk. He was a founder member of the Hospital Friends, driving and then organising the service, and would also regularly be found assisting me in whatever capacity was required, whether she was involved with Guides, the Hospital Friends or the Ardgowan Hospice ... even the Rankin.

In between times Bernard found time to write of his many adventures and experiences, starting with those in his youth and continuing with those of his seagoing career. He was introduced to Mr Brown, Editor of the *Nautical Magazine*, the periodical which regularly published Bernard's stories.

When he developed secondary form cancer we moved to a garden flat with a gorgeous view over the Clyde, where he spent much of his time sitting by the window, writing. We had a great celebration on his ninetieth birthday with his family, followed a few days later with another given by our special friends from the hospice. He died six months later on 4 March 1995, just before his fifteenth story was published. He was a

great person and backed up his family. I was his first
priority.

21

The Macular Disease Society

For sometime now I have been required to have regular check-ups in conjunction with the eyesight problem that has plagued me for the last few years, macular disease, deterioration of my central vision. In people of my age group the disease is not uncommon, and like it or not is just something that you require to live with, as at the moment there is no known effective cure for the condition.

When it was diagnosed, Dr David Mansfield, Consultant Ophthalmologist at Inverclyde Royal Hospital, Greenock advised me that it might be helpful for me to join and attend meetings of the Macular Disease Society support group which were held in Glasgow once a month. The meetings would be informative and might help me to come to terms with my deteriorating eyesight problem.

I duly went along to the next meeting in Nye Bevan House in Glasgow and was made most welcome. Several months later a major Scottish conference was being held by the Macular Disease Society in Dunfermline, and when I mentioned to Dr Mansfield my intention to attend, he was most interested and intimated his desire to be informed of the outcome at my next clinic.

My next clinic was in November 2003, and during consultation Dr David Mansfield asked if I had attended the conference in Dunfermline. I informed him that I had and that it had been a very good event. One of the topics discussed was the need for an increase in the number of local support groups. Before I could say anything else he commented, "Well, Marion, there's got to be a group right here in Greenock." To say I was taken slightly aback is an understatement, and, to be honest, he made me feel a bit of a worm. At that the consultation finished and I was ushered out of the room.

When I had finished sorting out a date for my next appointment and generally getting myself organised, another patient, completely unknown to me, informed me that she had just seen Dr Mansfield and he had informed her, "We are going to set up a local support group in Inverclyde." The lady thought this was just wonderful. I must say that I did not really feel the same way; I felt as if I had been slightly compromised, to say the least.

On the road home I gave the matter some thought and decided that if I was going to do anything about the matter I would need some help, the first thing being, where could such a meeting be held. Undaunted, I made a phone call to Mr Alan Burns, an old contact and friend who was employed by the local council Social Work Department. Alan listened to my concerns and informed me, "That is not a problem, Marion, you could hold meetings here at our Social Work Centre for the Disabled at Glenburn." Well, now at least I had a venue if I was going to carry on and get things organised.

I gave the matter some further thought, and the following Sunday, while at church, I mentioned my problem to one of the Elders whose wife happens to be totally blind. Mr Ian Wilkins and his wife May were sympathetic as far as my predicament was concerned, but nothing more was said at the time. After some more thought I contacted one of my old work colleagues from my Rankin Hospital days, Ruth Gillies, who once again was sympathetic, especially when I informed her of Dr Mansfield's insistence. Ruth informed me that she would give it some thought but was not all that keen to get too involved as she had not long retired and was enjoying the break from routine.

Several days later Ian Wilkins telephoned me and informed me that after some discussion with his wife, May, he would be available to give me assistance to get a group off the ground and was prepared to act as Secretary / Treasurer until such time as A.N. Other could be found. I contacted Ruth once again and managed to get her agreement to come along to my flat and have a discussion with Ian and myself to see if we could get things moving. By the time of the meeting in early December I had also managed to involve Mrs Margaret Gatherer, another resident within the block of flats where I live, who also has eye problems... The band was now four.

Alan Burns managed along to the initial planning meeting as well, and before long not only did we have a meeting venue but we also had limited copying facilities and any other support that the Visually Impaired Social Work team could provide. It was agreed at that meeting that we would all go along to the next Macular Group meeting being held in Glasgow the following week and get some idea as to how things were run and the type of meetings that were held, The four of us also went along to the meeting in the January of 2004 for good measure, and the support and encouragement we received was unbelievable; the Glasgow team could not do enough to help us get off the ground.

A starter information pack was received from the national headquarters of the Macular Disease Society in Andover, and with the help of Sue Wood we had the national body behind us as well. A list of all the known members of the national body in our area was produced and sent off by Sue, which allowed Ian to write to those concerned and send out an invitation to attend the new group.

Our first meeting was held at the old Glenburn School, Greenock on the second Wednesday of February 2004, and I was totally surprised by the numbers that turned out on the day. The Visually Impaired staff, in conjunction with Ruth and Margaret, were running around dispensing tea and coffee to all who wished refreshment, and the chatter among the participants was heartening to say the least, so much so that it took our first speaker Ms Mary Reilly from

Visibility in Glasgow all her time to be able to be heard over the noise – a most successful meeting with some 20-plus attending.

We started off that first meeting with a deficit of £64 by the time we had sorted out the costs for stationery and postage; however, the support we received and the £1 per head levy that was placed on each participant helped to soften the financial blow. Staff Nurse Kathryn Rankin also managed to get away from her morning clinic at the hospital on the day and was soon involved chatting to a lot of the people she normally saw as patients.

The meeting also allowed the Social Work team of Patricia Lafferty and Fiona McInnes the opportunity to get first hand contact with some people they had not managed to visit in recent months. All in all it was a worthwhile exercise.

A further meeting was held at the same venue on the second Wednesday of March 2004, which gave Alan Burns an opportunity to outline the work carried out by his department within the Inverclyde area. This meeting was followed up by another in April, but this time the venue changed to a new location at Inverclyde Council's Centre for Independent Living in Gibshill Road, Greenock, which is now our permanent monthly home.

As I write this some eighteen months after the initial start, I can hardly believe just how much has happened in the intervening months. We now hold meetings at Gibshill Road on the second Wednesday of every month, with the exception of July, August and

December. Up to now we have held a total of 15 monthly meetings whose speakers have included a fair number of macular related topics as well as representatives from R.N.I.B. and the local emergency services. This summer we held the first of what is hoped to be a regular feature, a bus run. On this occasion it was to a large garden centre in Ayr and proved very popular. We also managed to arrange a Christmas meal last year in the James Watt College in Greenock, which was also very popular – we must be doing something right, as the monthly attendance is getting closer to 40 persons each month.

Ian, my secretary / treasurer, is a lot happier as there is close to £1,000 in the bank now, the deficit having been paid off a long time ago, thanks mainly to the efforts of Staff Nurse Kathryn Rankin and her family, who secured a large amount of donations on the group's behalf from school fundraising to marathon running. In addition, numerous generous donations have been received on a regular basis from the membership as well as their regular monthly £1 fee.

In January 2004 we held our first A.G.M., which for a business meeting was very well attended, and were able, among other things to elect a 12 person steering committee to assist in the general business and meeting admin and organisation. Mrs Glynis Kerr and Mr Ian Forbes, spouses of two of our committee, were also included in this core team and both deputise as and when required.

At the moment several of the membership are in the process of undergoing training in what in macular terms is referred to as 'Eccentric Reading', the use of a specific type of magnifying spectacle which allows patients to use what peripheral vision they still have available. At the end of the training period they will not be able to read *War and Peace,* but enough vision of a sort is available to them which allows the reading of the morning mail or part of the daily newspaper, which apart from all else gives then some form of independence and goes even further in raising their hopes and self-esteem.

The cause of macular disease in Inverclyde is being served well. Without the varied support I receive, however, it would not be possible.

As usual, I did not go looking for it – it came to me!

22

The Burma Star Association

2005 Return

I was persuaded to join the Burma Star Association rather late in the day by Mr Albert Godfrey of Houston. When asked why I had not joined earlier I replied, "Because nobody asked me," and that is the truth. Still, 2003 was a good year for both them and me; after all it was nearly 60 years to the day from the time I earned the right to wear the emblem.

Albert Godfrey was very supportive, despite being blind and in a wheelchair, and just a few weeks later insisted that I join the Group for a commemoratory parade and service in Dunoon. So I got out the old medals, gave them a bit of spit and polish, wrapped myself up warmly and off I went, and lo and behold, I ended up, along with Godfrey, in the front of the parade. They were so pleased to see me and find out as much as they could about my service life that I began to feel like the Regimental Mascot.

Since that time I have managed to attend meetings in Paisley and Perth and have spent many hours reminiscing on that part of another time when the grass was not as worn and policemen were not as young as they are today.

On these occasions I also had the opportunity to come into contact with Sir Eric Yarrow once again, who during the writing of this book has been very supportive indeed.

At some point during 2004, I was asked if I might consider joining one of the groups which were being recruited to take part in a return trip to the Burma Theatre for the 60th Anniversary of V.J. Day in 2005. Once I found out the details I sounded out one or two people to gauge opinion as to whether I should risk it at my age. The main one was my doctor who had no hesitation, followed by my elder son John, who in fact agreed to come on the journey with me if I decided in the end that I was actually up for it, as they say nowadays.

When I got over the shock of the costs involved and discovered that I might be eligible for some grant finance through the Heroes Return Fund, to ease the pain, the day seemed to brighten, and the more I discussed it with my social circle I received nothing but support, and even offers from some to smuggle themselves into my luggage.

As it turned out the funding was considerable, and John managed to arrange holidays, so off we set for an overnight stay in London on Thursday 10 March 2005. The following morning 100 of us set off for Rangoon via Bangkok in a very different and faster mode of transport than the last time we went. On arrival we were billeted in the Dusit Inya Hotel, which was complete with ponds, wildlife and beautiful tropical flowers in the spacious gardens.

On the Saturday, we attended British Legion organised Services of Remembrance at both the Htaukkyan and Rangoon War Cemeteries as well as a Remembrance Service in Rangoon Cathedral in the afternoon, all of which were attended by a Burmese Minister, the representatives of each group, government representatives and the British Ambassador, H.E. Mrs Vicky Bowman. Wreathes were laid, and we all had bunches of poppies to lay at the Cross. We also visited a smaller R.A.F. cemetery. In all there were rows of small headstones with the details of each man inscribed, surrounded by lovely plants and flowers. We had small crosses to plant as well. The services were very moving and brought many tears to bowed heads. Later in the evening we all attended a reception at the British Ambassador's residence, which gave further opportunity to engage in recounting individual tales of our wartime experiences. In some cases stories were told for the first time.

The following morning being Sunday, we had an opportunity to return to the cemeteries to carry out visitations of a private and individual nature – very moving indeed.

Later in the day we carried out a visit to the Schwedega Pagoda, which was a big area with a great number of pagodas, all covered in gold and for different needs. Hundreds were kneeling and offering gifts at various pagodas praying for their needs. We went round in bare feet.

On the Monday we broke up into our separate groups. In our group there were twenty and we flew to Akyab, now Sittwe, one of the places where we had taken on casualties. It is a poor area, where the local mode of transport is Raleigh bicycles.

On the Tuesday and Wednesday the twenty of us went north up the River Mayu via Rathedaung to Buthidaung on a riverboat, and tied up at various places where battles had taken place. Old soldiers told their story and laid a small cross. I realised that when we nursed these men they never spoke of their awful experiences. At one of our stops we were driven overland to the Tunnels. Both nights were spent on board ship.

During one of these stops I came across Bert, who was on his own by the river bank, just sitting, deep in his thoughts, very deep in his thoughts. I stood beside him quietly for quite a while and eventually he recounted some of his stories. He told me what had happened, and the fact that in one particular case our lot had blown up a bridge to ensure the Japanese could not make use of it – the only thing was that a large number of our lads were still on the wrong side of the bridge and had no chance of getting across before it was destroyed. As Bert said, "We saw to the wounded, then buried the dead, that was all you could do." Tears were streaming down his face. Very quietly we both marked the spot with our little crosses. This type of thing was experienced many times over the two-day period. Very moving, but borne with a very British resolve.

The pair of us chatted further, and at one point he informed me that he had been wounded and taken to Chittagong on a hospital ship. I asked him if he had been moved on a train at night; he said he had. He told me a nice Sister had placed him on a veranda, in his stretcher, and then he told me he remembered being tied onto his stretcher and lifted onto the hospital ship. By this time I had started to laugh. He then commented about the ship having a very nice Chief Officer; at that I really laughed and then informed him that he had been on board Hospital Ship No. 6 and that the nice Sister was me, and that the Chief Officer became my husband – it's a small world. The Burmese were delightful, we were made so welcome. When we sailed away from the village hundreds waved and cheered, calling, "Come back soon!" They need more visitors and trade, but European governments do not approve of the present Burmese government, which is corrupt, and does not help the ordinary folk.

We returned to the same hotel in Rangoon via Akyab on the Thursday and then spent the Friday and most of Saturday generally sightseeing, as we had the time to ourselves.

Later on the Saturday we departed from Rangoon in the early evening, arriving in Bangkok just before 10.00 p.m., and a couple of hours later we were London bound once more.

All in all a very hectic eleven days, all of which my son John and I would not have missed for the world. In John's case he had the opportunity to visit locations he had heard of all his life, but actually seeing the places and hearing the reminiscences from those who were able to impart their tales has left a lasting impression and also a form of closure to a lot of things.

For my part, being a reasonably new recruit to the Association, I was honoured to be included, and at the same time humbled by their genuine comradeship. Yes, like all the others I had my moments, I would not have expected anything less, especially in an area where my wonderful Bernard and I spent so much of our younger years, infused with the hazards of the wartime Far East.

I'm glad I went back, very glad, and grateful that the good Lord allowed me to do so.

In August of this year of the 60th Anniversary, accompanied by my son Roger, I attended the official Scottish parade to mark the occasion, which was held in Aberdeen in the presence of H.R.H. Prince Philip, Duke of Edinburgh. Once again it was good to meet with the old comrades and join them in this act of Remembrance, which was led by Sir Eric Yarrow.

While there, I came across another gentleman who informed me that he still had vivid memories of being one of numerous casualty evacuees who was transported in the S.S. *Wusueh* from Maundaw to Chittagong. The heartache and the memories don't fade; the difficulty is finding someone to listen to them who was there at the time and went through the same life-changing experiences – they are the only ones who really understand.

Like a lot of others, I get the feeling that we are still the 'Forgotten Army', especially when the true date of our anniversary was not used for this last major parade.

I am honoured, nevertheless, to wear the Burma Star Association and War Veterans Badges – we earned them!

Appendix 1: Historical Note

This summary of events appeared on the Order of Service at an event attended by the author, and is to be found on the website of the Burma Star Association http://www.burmastar.org.uk/notes.htm .
It is reprinted here with the permission of the Association.

The war in the Far East started in December 1941, simultaneously with the bombing of Pearl Harbour. The Japanese captured Hong Kong on Christmas Day and moved into the Malaysian Peninsula, the Philippines and the Dutch East Indies. Malaya was overrun and Singapore fell on 15 February 1942. The Japanese army advanced into Burma, involving the defending British and Indian troops in a long and demoralising fighting retreat through thick jungle terrain over a distance equivalent to that from Istanbul to London. Rangoon fell on 8 March 1942, and by mid-June the Japanese advance had reached the hills on the North East frontier of India.

In December 1942, British and Indian troops mounted their first offensive in the malaria ridden coastal Arakan region. It was unsuccessful, although much was learned. During 1943, Chindit columns under Brigadier Orde Wingate, supported by the Royal Air Force, penetrated deep behind the Japanese lines in central Burma. In March 1943, a further determined attempt to invade India was repulsed after fierce fighting. In August 1943 the South East Asia Command was formed under Lord Louis Mountbatten and in October that year General William Slim was appointed as Commander of the Fourteenth Army.

In March 1944, the Japanese launched an offensive across the Chindwin River, cutting the Imphal–Kohima Road. There followed the ferocious battles of the 'Admin Box', Kohima (with its famous tennis court) and Imphal, at the end of which the defeated Japanese withdrew. Further Chindit columns operated deep behind enemy lines during 1944 and at the beginning of 1945 the Fourteenth Army launched a successful offensive down the Arakan Coast, followed by a major advance deep into central Burma. Mandalay was retaken on 20 March after a twelve day battle, and the Fourteenth Army continued on to Rangoon, which was reoccupied in an amphibious operation on 3 May.

The Fourteenth Army, known to many as 'The Forgotten Army', numbered over one million men under arms, the largest Commonwealth army ever assembled. Air lines of communication were crucial; some 615,000 tons of supplies and 315,000 reinforcements were airlifted to and from the front line, frequently by parachuted air drops, and 210,000 casualties were evacuated. The Royal Air Force and the Indian Air Force, supported by carrier-borne Fleet Air Arm aircraft, provided constant offensive bombing sorties, together with fighter cover and essential photo-reconnaissance in support of the Army. Towards the end of the War, R.A.F. Liberator aircraft carried out some of the longest operations ever flown to drop mines into the Pacific. At sea, the Royal Navy and the Royal Indian Navy provided the landing craft, the minesweeping operations and the combined operations necessary for the coastal offensive in the Arakan, as well as providing gunfire support from seaward. The Royal Marine Commando, as well as Royal Marines from the units of the Fleet, took part in the Arakan operations.

The Japanese surrendered on 15 August 1945, now known as V.J. Day.

Appendix 2: Maps

India

Burma

Venezuela

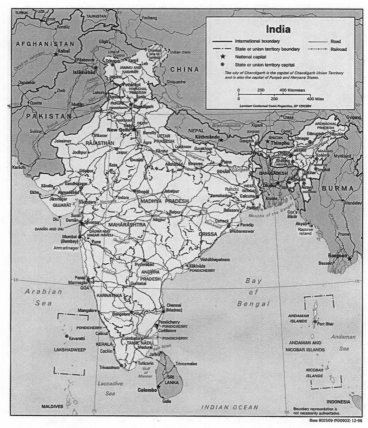

9th C.C.S. and Burmese Operational Area.
Reprinted by courtesy of the University of Texas Libraries,
The University of Texas at Austin.

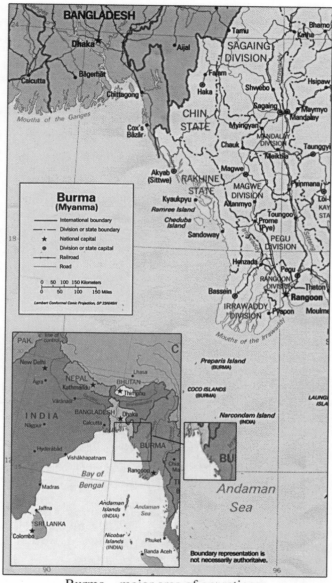

Burma – major area of operations.
Reprinted by courtesy of the University of Texas Libraries,
The University of Texas at Austin.

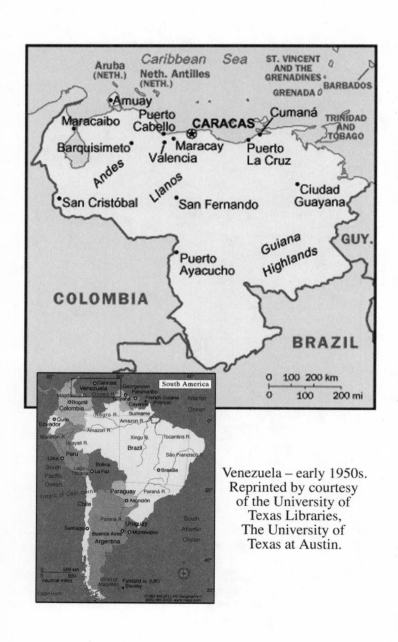

Venezuela – early 1950s.
Reprinted by courtesy
of the University of
Texas Libraries,
The University of
Texas at Austin.